A Parent's Survival Guide

For the Parent of
The Elite Pitcher

by

Coach Ron Wolforth

Coach Wolforth's
Survival Guide for the Parent of the Elite Pitcher
Copyright © 2013 by Ron Wolforth's Texas Baseball Ranch LLC

ISBN 978-0615705286
Printed in the United States of America

We Have Found a Hidden Treasure

"Ron Wolforth's genius is not in his deep knowledge and understanding of pitching (though profound). It abides in his willingness and ability to take a very complex physiological process & communicate it to anyone who is motivated to learn. This is non-existent in baseball today and is testimony to his love of the game, but more importantly, his passion for helping others. He shares his incredible gift with infectious joy... We have found a hidden treasure and it resides in Montgomery, Texas."

Jim Davidson, Father of Elite Pitcher
Holland, PA

"Wolforth is an extraordinary coach and a master teacher. His thirst for knowledge, and creative thinking are truly inspiring. His approach is based on truth and not tradition. This book is the result of his quest for excellence. **Within these pages you will find everything you need for proper pitching**

mechanics, philosophy, and execution. I highly recommend this book and will be teaching these throwing principles to my own children."

Raul Ibanez
17 Year Major League Player
2009 All-Star

"Relying on first-hand experience, in this type of arena, can be quite costly. Imagine if you could avoid injury for your son's arm, or body? Would you want him to "learn the hard way"? Baseball is a game that requires a ton of perspective from a parent's viewpoint. All that matters when your son is 12, or 16, or 18 is that along the development curve he has a chance to reach his potential. Regardless of what that potential ceiling is, relying on first-hand knowledge with the possibility of injury and ineffectiveness is not secure.

As a kid, I was a great reader, and from A-Z it seemed like I'd read every available book on pitching, even skimming biographies for inspiration. I never got my hands on Ron's method until I was already in the major leagues, which by that time I'd already had enough injuries to essential body parts. Perhaps if my family and myself could rewind the clock, then I might have been able to avoid some of the injuries and their lasting effects.

A saying you learn in the minor leagues: nobody gets sent to the big leagues from the training room.

Find a way to make yourself stronger, more stable mechanically, and mentally by working on the right program and having a bit of perspective. It's more important to improve, and if you are going for the top, you better do what you can to keep yourself in one piece."

C.J. Wilson
Major League Picher, Los Angeles Angels
2011 American League All-Star

"I started with Coach Wolforth after my freshman year of high school. I was fourteen at the time and came to The Ranch, which was still known as Can-Am at the time, throwing 78 miles per hour. **One year later, after attending two boot camps and three weeks of summer session at The Ranch, I hit 94 in a game.** *The jump in velocity was great, as it helped me get noticed and continue playing baseball at the next level, but the best part about The Ranch, to me, is the wealth of information and lack of ego associated with training there. Coach Wolforth has a true commitment to getting it "right" regardless of who comes up with the information or ideas. I have been training with Ron for close to 8 years now. In those eight years I have seen the program morph, evolve and improve constantly, incorporating all areas important to becoming a successful pitcher. Some of these include: velocity, command, arm health, arm strength, mental preparation, physical preparation and pitch sequencing. I am blessed to have gotten to know Coach Wolforth when I did and consider my time around him and those who practice his program to be the only reason I am still playing baseball today."*

Trevor Bauer
2011 Golden Spikes Award Winner
#3 Draft Pick 2011 Draft, Arizona Diamondbacks

*"**If you are looking for a magic formula to create your athlete into an elite athlete, don't buy this book.**"*

"Coach Wolforth has created a system that requires hard work, commitment and perseverance to help a person succeed in meeting their goal of becoming an elite athlete.

Nearly three years ago our son went to his first Wolforth camp and he was hooked immediately. Coach Wolforth is a combination of motivational speaker; task master and tell it like it is guy who truly believes that ANYONE can achieve their goal, as long as they are willing to adjust their mindset and work harder than they ever have before.

The Elite Pitcher series was exactly what our son was looking for to increase his arm strength and velocity. We had looked at many different types of throwing programs, but no other program really dove deep into the details of the why and how to actually achieve success. In addition, Coach Wolforth includes the mental approach in his program, which is so critical to the success of young athletes.

Fast forward two and a half years, and our son's throwing velocity has increased over 25 mph using Wolforth's program and attending Wolforth camps. The funniest thing about the increase in his arm strength is: our son is NOT a pitcher—he is a catcher! The arm strength, speed and velocity increases created by this program are not just for pitchers.

We are grateful to Coach Wolforth for his Elite Pitcher program and the interest he has taken in the development of our son as both an athlete and as a young man. Thanks Coach!"

Maureen & Mark Juaire
Farmington, MN

"Who can you trust? Who can you believe? Where can you get information based on experience and research? As parents we all want the best experience for our children. We look for the 'best' coach for our young players, the 'best' team, the 'best' school to attend, etc.

Coach Wolforth takes the guesswork out of these questions. Coach has a wealth of experience and a program based on research and proven results. As a parent of a baseball player you will find these concerns given clear and thoughtful responses in 'Parents Survival Guide.'

It is tough out there to get advice and direction you can trust - Coach Wolforth has the track record and the information you need to lead you and your young players in a positive direction."

Pat Doyle
Global Coordinator,
Envoy Coach Program
Major League Baseball
1999 - 2012

44 years coaching in High
School, Community College,
USA National Team,
International Baseball and
youth baseball

"*My experience with Ron and The Baseball Ranch has really opened my eyes and mind to a wealth of baseball and mechanical knowledge that I had not known even existed. Ron has dedicated his time and will to uncover the truth of healthy pitching mechanics.*

My velocity has escalated, my breaking balls have become sharper, my command is much more consistent, and I have The Texas Baseball Ranch to thank for that. It was definitely a challenge and isn't something that instantly clicks, but that's the beauty of it. You have to work, you have to want it, you have to have the desire to be something worthwhile.

It's amazing, what I thought was my full potential only to find I could tap into more. *What Ron has researched and taught me has helped me escalate through the minor leagues and looking at an MLB debut within the next couple years.*

I am only 20 years old and am so close to capturing my dream. I have Ron and The Ranch to thank for helping me realize what I am capable of doing, and now I am doing it."

Cody Buckel
Top Prospect, Texas Rangers

Table of Contents:

Part III. What is so unique about the philosophy of Ron Wolforth's Texas Baseball Ranch™ and what can you learn and how can you benefit from our processes?

Part IV. Final Pieces of Advice   129

Common Sense is unfortunately not common.

   - If you do what everybody else does…you are going to get what everybody else gets.
   - If you do what you've always done…you are going to get what you've always gotten.
   - The definition of insanity.
   - As with everything else in life, it all comes down to knowledge and education.
   - As with everything else in life, it all comes down to finding just the right person/expert/mentor.
   - As with everything else in life, it all comes down to ACTION vs. intentions, feelings or thoughts.

Bonus Section

Introduction

Ever since I was a little boy, I wanted to be a professional baseball player. When people asked me if I had a Plan B, my answer would always be "No. That would simply detract from Plan A." My parents had very little background in athletics. They were simple, small town, Midwestern folks who had very little influence, very few connections and very little understanding of how competitive athletics operated. That doesn't mean they were bad parents. But to everything there is a learning curve coupled with a very finite amount of time to figure things out. In that way, I had a huge disadvantage. My wife, Jill, can tell you a very similar story with her experience in softball and competitive athletics in college.

This book was designed with that learning curve and strict timetable in mind. My sincere hope is that this book will give you perspective and direction that you might otherwise not get. My goal is to shorten that learning curve and aid you and your athlete in his journey to be the best that he can be and achieve his dream.

Part I.

DANGER! DANGER! DANGER!

I'm afraid my athlete will get injured.

*Straight Talk From
America's "Go-To-Guy"
On Pitching*

1

Chapter 1

The Truth about Soft Tissue, Growth Plates and Injuries to Pitchers

Did it ever strike you as odd that a veteran major league pitcher, in essence a fully grown man with years of experience and supposedly "a sound movement pattern", will only throw 1-2 innings in his first outing in Spring Training, while it is not uncommon for a high school pitcher to throw a complete game in his very first game of the season or for the youth pitcher to throw his maximum allotment of 9 innings over his first weekend tournament?

It should.

It represents a real intellectual disconnect. From the time they are born until they are 25 years of age, most males are a literal growth machine. At no time is this growth more prevalent than during the ages 9-18. To allow for such amazing spurts and expansion, the soft tissue around the joints and growth plates are really put to the test; and that's without a young man doing anything out of the normal.

Enter competitive athletes and the desire to throw harder, run faster, jump higher, etc....ALL of this in an emotionally charged environment and THEN:

○   We are going to do this ALL year long with very little break...(Spring, Summer and Fall baseball)
○   Often play on two teams, one during the week and another on weekends.

o   Throw in a showcase or two.

o   Add in some mechanical inefficiencies and/or immature movement patterns. *(Which ALMOST ALWAYS is the case. How could it not be? All of us start out as novices with immature movement patterns and they develop slowly and steadily over time. Yet somehow we think a 13-year-old has developed a world class, highly efficient movement pattern? I assure you that is almost NEVER the case... regardless of the perceived skill or competitive success of the athlete).*

o   Mix in a strength imbalance and perhaps a physical asymmetry or two.

o   Include mobility and/or flexibility constraint(s) or limitation(s) or two.

o   Factor in questionable nutrition, hydration, sleep and recovery.

What we have is the perfect storm. To be frank, it is amazing to me that even MORE youth pitching athletes don't require medical/surgical intervention these days.

Time for Some Straight Talk and
Some Harsh Reality

On top of being a professional pitching instructor, I am a parent of an elite baseball player and for the past year now, a grandparent. There are a few realities that we as parents and grandparents all need to come to grips with and understand as we begin our discussion about our pitching athletes.

The youth pitchers who are almost always at the greatest risk of injury are the harder throwing kids. Not only does he have more energy going through his system and therefore more potential stress to soft tissue, he just as obviously will be called upon to pitch more frequently and also will be left in the games he does pitch for greater periods of time. He is more likely to be extended in the postseason when winning really matters to the select/travel ball or high school coach.

He will be coveted far more by other teams and therefore will pitch more often on additional teams who will ask him to play in "extra" tournaments/showcases and camps. (*After all, what young man and his parents wouldn't love to be wanted and highly sought after?*)

The Universe Has Changed Dramatically since 1969

The universe of youth sports has changed dramatically since I was a 9-year-old and began pitching in 1969; and no matter how much we long for times long past, they are never coming back.

Gone are the 15-30 game seasons over 3 months in the summer. Here to stay are far more games (often over 100), over far more months (10-12 months out of the year).

It was fairly uncommon to see an 85+ mph pitcher in high school in the 1970's. Today it is almost a necessity to throw with that velocity to even have an opportunity to pitch for the better high schools in California, Florida, Arizona, Texas and the rest of the Deep South.

To be taken into account for the major league draft, the standard for high school and college pitchers has also steadily increased until today many pitchers throwing in excess of 92 mph will not even be considered by MLB organizations.

Bottom line: Velocity is coveted by athletes, for the very reason that velocity is coveted by coaches at every level. Young athletes and their supporters will actively look for ways to throw with more velocity. And in fact that is exactly what has happened:

The average velocity at every level is going up. Therefore, although very few are saying it, stress to soft tissue is of course going up as well.

Therefore in this day and age, parents and athletes have two primary choices:

1) Stay safe and be passed over by other athletes willing to risk injury;
2) Or risk injury themselves.

As the bar for entry into top level baseball gets set higher and higher, the risk of injury to soft tissue and growth plates also increases.

Once parents and athletes decide they are willing to "go for it", the risk of injury to the young pitcher becomes a fact of life. Many parents and athletes are either naive about those risks or have chosen to stick their head in the proverbial sand and hope everything will turn out all right.

As we often say at the Texas Baseball Ranch: "Hope is NOT a plan!"

If your athlete has decided pitching a baseball is something he is truly serious about, then preparing his soft tissue for the stress it will encounter, improving mechanical efficiencies, managing workloads and paying attention to growth plate issues, growth spurts, tenderness, tightness and pain is not only a good idea but mandatory due diligence. Gone are the days where you could just wing it. Well, I guess you could try to wing it, many actually do, but the results are most often far from satisfying.

Welcome to the world of competitive youth athletics circa 2013. It is a world where an athlete's soft tissue and growth plates are put under tremendous stress. Some may tell you it shouldn't be like this and if we would only legislate out bad coaches, curveballs and radar guns and legislate in pitch counts, time off and "good mechanics" (*more on this topic in Chapter #5*), everyone would be safer, healthier and fantastic!

However, I don't live in utopia. I train athletes in the real world. Paying close attention to growth spurts and pain/tightness/tenderness is critical. A systematic preparation of soft tissue for the stress it will be placed under is absolutely essential. Cleaning up mechanical inefficiencies is imperative. Managing workloads, scheduling down time and focusing on recovery only makes good common sense.

Wishing for an ideal environment or lamenting that situations are not copacetic, on the other hand, is a giant waste of time in my opinion. It has us expending energy on the wrong things. Here at the Texas Baseball Ranch we expend our energy on the variables we can affect.

And as Robert Frost once wrote:

> "Two roads diverged in a wood and I—
> I took the one less traveled by
> and that has made all the difference."

 I've prepared something very special for my readers that will assist you in continuing your elite pitcher experience. Download Your Free Report:

"Why 95% of Pitchers Fail and How You Can Avoid Being One of Them"
At: **www.TexasBaseballRanch.com**

Summary Notes of this chapter for the Parent:

- ✓ Pay close attention to growth spurts; it is during these spurts when your athlete is at a greater risk of injury.
- ✓ Pay very close attention to complaints of pain, discomfort, tenderness, tightness, even simple fatigue. These are signals from the body for attention. Do not simply disregard these signs as a common by-product of the activity. Reject the "don't ask, don't tell" approach to arm pain.
- ✓ The kids MOST at risk are the harder throwers.
- ✓ The kids MOST at risk are the ones that pitch year round and/or who pitch in both a league and on weekend tournaments.
- ✓ It is a fact of life that velocity is coveted and that fact is never going to go away.
- ✓ Parents and athletes have a choice to make:
    - o Stay safe and be passed over by other athletes willing to risk injury
    - o Or risk injury themselves
- ✓ If your athlete has decided pitching a baseball is something he is serious about, then preparing his soft tissue for the stress it will encounter, improving mechanical efficiencies, managing workloads and paying attention to growth plate issues, growth spurts, tenderness, tightness and pain is not only a good idea but mandatory due diligence.

Coach Wolforth's Recommendations:

- Do not pitch year round. I recommend participating in multiple sports for as long as an athlete possibly can. You can throw a baseball year round, but I strongly recommend taking off from competitive pitching at minimum 6 months of the year.

- Do not pitch in multiple leagues. Choose to pitch either during the week or during the weekend, not both. While I wouldn't recommend playing in both leagues, playing in them is far different than pitching in both leagues. I will state again. Do NOT pitch in multiple leagues.

- Prepare for the stress of pitching. Resting is NOT preparation. Resting is recuperation. These are two totally different things. The preparation I'm referring to is the training of the entire body for the specific demands and requirements involved in high level competition. Injuries come from being underprepared for the specific demands of intensity or workload involved.

- Make it a priority to improve your pitching athlete's mechanical efficiency, especially his ability to decelerate.

- If you must, take control of managing your athlete's pitching workloads. I realize many of you think this is outside your ability to control lest you be given the moniker of "psycho over-involved parent". In my opinion, you must become educated regarding workloads and become engaged if the coaches involved do not understand or disregard workloads. How well you articulate your concerns and the willingness of the coach to hear reasonable, well-stated concerns is of course another matter entirely.

- Really educate yourself in the processes of recovery for your pitcher. Many injuries are created or exacerbated by an athlete who has not adequately recovered from his previous throwing workload.

- Teach your athlete to "shut it down" immediately if anything feels odd, uniquely uncomfortable or painful. I remind you that this particular game or tournament, however it is being defined by other coaches, players and parents, is NOT more important than the long-term health of your young athlete.

- If your athlete complains of pain anywhere in the soft tissue of the elbow or shoulder, it is a sign of a weak link, disconnection and/or mechanical inefficiency. Seek immediate expert advice or contact our office in Texas.

Chapter 2

The Truth about Curveballs, Sliders and Cutters

I'm certain by now, if you are a parent of even an 8-year-old pitcher, you've heard many of the horror stories about curveballs. In fact, one nationally known orthopedic surgeon who is the team orthopedic for an MLB team has even called for the banning of ALL curveballs and sliders in prepubescent male populations. This doctor even went as far as calling for the ejection and suspension of pitchers and coaches who utilize any form of breaking ball in an organized game. Many in the media and others inside of medicine have applauded and echoed his "principled" stand. As injuries to youth pitchers increase, in my opinion the clamoring for legislation to protect the youth will inevitably increase as well.

So am I really going to "Cross the Rubicon" and dare to disagree with such experts? You bet your sweet "bippie" I will. If I don't stand up to this pomposity, who is going to? Sticking to my river analogy, this doctor, in my opinion, in an effort to sound like the smartest, most concerned guy on the planet, has actually traveled a couple bridges too far; and like many other past attempts of well-intended legislation, not only will it not solve the problem but such a law would inject several unintended negative consequences into the situation.

Here is what I believe is common sense about breaking balls in the prepubescent male pitcher. It is straightforward but multifaceted; and in the end, it is simple but not easy. How about that for a preface? I hope you have a sense of humor because in the training of complex movement patterns of young people, you are going to need it.

Let me walk you through breaking balls and why, in my opinion, it has gotten such a bad reputation.

Fact #1. One of the two primary places in the delivery where the stress on the medial elbow is at its greatest is right at release when the olecranon fossa can bang into the olecranon process. In the pictures below, the pitcher on the left is a youth pitcher throwing a fastball and the one on the right a youth pitcher throwing a breaking ball.

Fastball at release	Breaking ball at release

Fact #2. The way the arm naturally and most efficiently decelerates is for the forearm/hand to pronate immediately after launch. At The Ranch we actually refer to it as "pronating into launch" implying that effective pronation/deceleration is simply part of the launch process. As you can see in 3 of the 4 pictures on this page, the ball is just out of the hand and the pronation has already occurred.

| Roy Oswalt pronation | Matt Cain pronation |

| Cliff Lee pronation | Tim Lincecum pronation |

Fact #3. If the pitcher releases the baseball out in front of his body with the throwing shoulder significantly out in front of the glove side/directional shoulder, the arm will decelerate much more efficiently and the bang of the olecranon fossa into the olecranon process is minimal or nonexistent.

Roger Clemens at ball release

Roy Oswalt at ball release

Fact #4. The curveball, at release, represents the most supinated orientation possible, thereby requiring the most time to pronate and thereby the most time to decelerate most efficiently.

Steven Strasburg throwing a breaking ball at ball release

Fact #5. Most youth pitchers are inefficient in their mechanics and tend to begin their rotation very early; therefore a vast majority of them fail to release the baseball significantly out in front and subsequently do not pronate/decelerate efficiently, adding significant stress to soft tissue in elbow and shoulder.

Young pitcher with premature rotation/ early launch

Fact #6. Every prepubescent pitcher's growth plates are wide open for stretches of their early baseball career, so their soft tissue and bone are already more at risk from the stress of throwing a baseball at high speed.

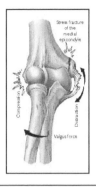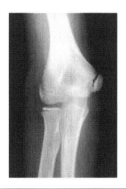

Examples of the complexity of the
structure of the elbow

Fact #7. Most youth pitchers have alignment asymmetries, strength imbalances and mobility/flexibility constraints or limitations which will complicate any movement pattern, so their soft tissue and bone are already more at risk from stress of throwing a baseball at high end point velocities.

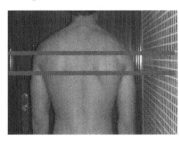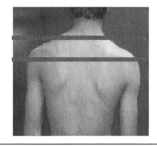

Examples of asymmetries and imbalances which
complicate any movement pattern.

Fact #8. Many youth pitchers are taught the curveball incorrectly and are taught instead to manipulate or "turn" the curveball, making the efficient deceleration/pronation of the arm even more difficult; in fact, sometimes the incorrect instruction literally makes an efficient deceleration impossible.

 If you are unsure of the proper way to throw a curveball, safely and efficiently, I strongly recommend this DVD from Brent Strom. **'Brent Strom's Enhancing the Curveball'** is available at: **www.PitchingCentral.com**

Fact #9. Many youth pitchers fall in love with the pitch and throw 40-60% breaking balls because the hitters they face at their level usually have little experience hitting curveballs and they get easily fooled by such a pitch.

So in truth the curveball itself is simply ONE of many mitigating factors to the injury to youth pitchers and when everything is considered, one of the more insignificant

factors, in my opinion. <u>In essence the curveball/slider/cutter</u> <u>makes the deceleration of the arm more complicated.</u> While things which complicate an already inefficient and immature movement pattern are obviously not a great idea, it is not nearly enough to warrant banning the curveball or promoting it as the primary cause of injury. In my opinion, such a call for action is an overreaction and represents a significant inferential leap.

I have had many parents boast "And my Johnny, who is now 16, has never been allowed to throw a curveball," believing that this one move has saved their child from risk of injury. Unfortunately, in my opinion, such a stand is more "fool's gold" than anything else and represents a lack of understanding of the real threat. It would be akin to a parent bragging that they have an absolute zero tolerance regarding smoking in their house while they pay no attention to the liquor cabinet or to their child driving home late from an unsupervised party.

Eliminating the curveball in games, in my opinion, will have very, very little impact on injuries and will introduce other elements into the game which will be horrific—like amateur umpires determining if a pitcher actually threw a breaking ball or a slip/split change up (they have their hands full with strike/ball and safe/out already) and coaches and players trying to scam or stretch the new rule to their advantage.

I simply shudder to think of how going in such a direction would play out.

Let's take the average 12-year-old boy:
-This young man has a few structural asymmetries and strength imbalances.

17

-Because of these he often has a less than ideal humeral orientation in his shoulder (meaning the head of the humerus doesn't move ideally in the socket of the shoulder) and his scapular stabilization (refers to the shoulder blade and the muscles which help stabilize and decelerate the shoulder and arm) is underdeveloped or imbalanced so it doesn't fully support the workings of the arm at high speeds as it ideally should.

-His strength, conditioning, skill specific fitness and co-ordination are still developing, so he is often awkward and spastic.

-He is prone to significant growth spurts, seemingly almost overnight, making him even more uncoordinated for stretches of time.

-He is inefficient and unpolished in his movement patterns, often with wide variation in subsequent deliveries. He rotates early, causing the arm to disconnect and create what Dr. Mike Marshall refers to as "forearm bounce" and "forearm fly-out", putting exponential stress on his already vulnerable soft tissue.

-He loves pitching and wants to be the best on his team and in his neighborhood. He knows he must throw the ball harder than others in his peer group to obtain throwing opportunities.

-If he is successful, he will pitch in more games and probably max out his innings each weekend because select coaches try to keep the number of roster players to a minimum to avoid parents complaining about playing/pitching time. By the end of the tournament, often the team runs short of pitching and the best pitchers on the team invariably have to carry the load every weekend.

-Because of the incredible money that is involved, his baseball season is much longer than ever before, and young people will often play in leagues during the week and almost every weekend from March through August.

-Because the competition is so fierce, strike zones have also incrementally shrank over the past 10 years and now select 12-year-olds are pitching to strike zones not even seen in college 20 years ago, artificially elevating pitch counts.

So let me ask you, the reader, a question. Now that you are aware of just a sampling of the circumstances that can and are affecting the young pitching athlete, do you think it is wise to single out curveballs as the anathema to youth baseball?

After looking holistically at this issue, hopefully many of you now have a slightly different perspective on the curveball and can see why I believe that curveballs and the debate over them has become a distraction from the REAL problems.

If curveballs were simply the bugaboo that this one renowned orthopedic doctor is certain that they are, shouldn't the curveball be banned in ALL baseball, even MLB?

The truth is studies have shown that, thrown correctly, the curveball is no more stressful to the arm or elbow than is the fastball. I don't hear the clamoring for the fastball to be banned, but in reality a fastball can be just as dangerous.

As I write this, I can just imagine the angst of many on the other side of this issue while they are reading this chapter. I'm sure they will claim that I'm playing word games and that if I truly cared about kids I would join them in demanding that we should never add complexity to an already stressed system... i.e. Throw the curveball.

I hear their arguments. I truly do.

At The Texas Baseball Ranch, a young person must pass out of a minimum of 12 weeks of dedicated mechanical efficiency work, especially focusing on pronation and deceleration before we even begin to focus upon speeding up the arm, and 24 weeks before we introduce the teaching of anything off speed, starting with the straight change. So trust me; we don't just give lip service to potential injury and insist on the passage of some draconian rules supposedly laid down to protect kids. We truly care about our athletes' development and we put our training where our mouth is. We add complexity only after they have mastered certain mechanical efficiencies.

I wholeheartedly believe the curveball has become a distraction of sorts from the real problems that face youth pitchers; and unfortunately these days the curveball is often used as a political wedge issue to disparage others as being more concerned about winning than the health of young arms.

In my personal opinion, this type of rhetoric and posturing does little to forward the conversation. If we are truly interested in helping young arms stay healthy, we should look at the entire picture and affect as many of the primary variables to arm health that we possibly can. We waste our time sniping at each other about the curveball.

As I mentioned earlier and I want to reiterate here, the curveball simply makes the pronation/deceleration of the

arm more complicated. The curveball itself is not a major cause of arm issues in the USA in my opinion. Instead we should look at the problem from a 360°, holistic point of view.

<u>Summary Notes of this chapter for the Parent:</u>

- ✓ As injuries to youth pitchers increase, in my opinion the clamoring for legislation to protect the youth will inevitably increase—including legislation to ban the curveball. In my opinion, education/application and not legislation is the only true solution to reducing injuries.
- ✓ Well-intended legislation not only will not solve the problem but will almost certainly inject several unintended negative consequences into the situation.
- ✓ Fact #1. One of the two primary places in the delivery where the stress on the medial elbow is at its greatest is right at release when the olecranon fossa can bang into the olecranon process.
- ✓ Fact #2. The way the arm naturally and most efficiently decelerates is for the forearm/hand to pronate immediately after launch. At The Ranch we actually refer to it as "pronating into launch", implying that effective pronation/ deceleration is simply part of the launch process.
- ✓ Fact #3. If the pitcher releases the ball in front of his body with the throwing shoulder significantly out in front of the glove side/directional shoulder, the arm will decelerate much more efficiently and the bang of the olecranon fossa into the olecranon process is minimal or nonexistent.
- ✓ Fact #4. The curveball, at release, represents the most supinated orientation possible, thereby requiring the most time to pronate and thereby more time to decelerate most efficiently.
- ✓ Fact #5. Most youth pitchers are inefficient in their mechanics, tend to begin their rotation early; therefore a

vast majority of them fail to release the baseball significantly out in front and subsequently do not pronate/ decelerate efficiently, adding significant stress to soft tissue in elbow and shoulder.

✓ Fact #6. Every prepubescent pitcher's growth plates are wide open for stretches of their early baseball career, so their soft tissue and bone are already more at risk from the stress of throwing a baseball at high speed.

✓ Fact #7. Most youth pitchers have alignment asymmetries, strength imbalances and mobility/flexibility constraints or limitations which will complicate any movement pattern, so their soft tissue and bone are already more at risk from the stress of throwing a baseball at high end point velocities.

✓ Fact #8. Many youth pitchers are taught the curveball incorrectly and are taught instead to manipulate or "turn/ twist" the curveball, making the efficient deceleration/ pronation of the arm even more difficult. Sometimes the incorrect instructions literally make an efficient deceleration impossible.

✓ Fact #9. Many youth pitchers fall in love with the pitch and throw 40-60% breaking balls because the hitters they face at their level usually have little experience hitting curveballs and they get easily fooled by such a pitch.

✓ In truth, the curveball itself is simply ONE of many aggravating factors to the injury to youth pitchers and when everything is considered, one of the more insignificant factors. In essence the curveball/slider/cutter makes the deceleration of the arm more complicated. While anything which complicates an already inefficient and immature movement pattern is obviously not a great idea, it is not nearly enough to warrant banning the curveball or forwarding it as the primary cause of injury.

Coach Wolforth's Specific Recommendations:

- Have your athlete assessed by a physical therapist who works with high level athletes. If your athlete has muscular imbalances, weaknesses, mobility constraints or alignment issues, those must be corrected.

- Get your athlete in front of a competent pitching instructor that understands pronation and deceleration. WARNING: Very few really are competent in this area. Instead they mistakenly believe deceleration/pronation is 100% natural and is non-teachable. The truth is that deceleration is like breathing. While innately "natural", every pitcher can decelerate more efficiently. For some, that improvement can be career changing/saving.

- AFTER your pitcher learns to deliver the baseball with the throwing shoulder closer to the target than his glove side shoulder AND pronate into launch on his fastball THEN the next step is to learn to throw a curveball. The process will take months, possibly over a year, before the athlete is ready to incorporate a curveball into the game. The process may be the best investment you could make in your athlete's baseball career. Most young men simply won't have the patience or dedication to master this essential element.

- Don't let your pitcher fall in love with the breaking ball. Keep its use to a maximum of 25% of total pitches thrown. Your athlete's development of his fastball will always be the primary focus to his ascension.

- Realize the world at large (especially so-called experts) has already decided the curveball is horrible and is an abomination to youth baseball; and any attempt to counter that position with logic almost assuredly will not be received well. I suggest you don't waste your time and view your understanding simply as one of your edges.

Chapter 3

The Truth about Velocity

It is simply impossible to have a discussion about pitching which does not include, in at least some part of it, addressing velocity. While all of us intuitively realize a pitcher's velocity is far from the whole story with regards to his effectiveness, velocity has always been and will always remain a benchmark for comparison and ultimately for opportunity.

Some of the world rails against young pitchers being radared. They believe the radar gun is actually a force for evil and injury creation. Believe me when I tell you that stance is not overstated. Some people think of the radar gun as simply evil and an emphasis upon velocity creation/enhancement in youth pitchers is the very worst idea in a long line of bad ideas. Many of these people are orthopedic surgeons, physical therapists and former major league pitchers such as Tommy John.

Again, am I going to risk very vitriolic responses from these people by disagreeing with their basic paradigm? I believe it is vitally important for me to openly disagree regardless of the probable negative blowback. I sincerely believe their take could be even more detrimental than that of others who believe the radar gun is the be all and end all of pitching development.

The radar gun is a tool, nothing more, nothing less. And like any other tool, it can be used for development or it can be misused and even abused and become detrimental to development.

Likewise, pretending that velocity isn't a factor in performance or a prevalent selection criteria, keeping athletes and parents in the dark in regard to where their athlete stacks up against his peers in terms of velocity or convincing the athlete and/or his parents that utilizing the radar gun would inevitably lead the young man to an injury, is in my opinion even more abusive and erroneous than a coach or instructor simply being fixated on radar readings. As long as the person accurately reports the readings, the readings are simply an objective measure. They are neither good nor bad. Only the interpretation and subsequent application of those numbers actually has the power to influence and shape our training.

For example, let us say a 10-year-old kicks a soccer ball 28 miles per hour. I'm a baseball guy. I have absolutely no idea if that kick is inadequate, decent or world class. I need someone with experience of soccer kicks at the youth level to interpret that speed for me. However that tool almost certainly could be of benefit to me in giving feedback to a soccer team made up of 10-year-olds.

I for one, fully believe in and utilize tools which afford me and my clients an objective measure of their progress.

The prevalent thought from the "antiradar gun" population is that players will forgo mechanical considerations, conditioning, command, movement, change of speeds and become fanatical with regards to velocity and become preoccupied in attempting to beat/top their last radar gun reading, thereby putting themselves at grave risk.

I would freely admit that is certainly one possible scenario.

However, there are many different scenarios that can and do play out, including one I have witnessed first-hand many times over during my career. If a person is never measured by a radar gun or never measures his long toss for years, he might have very little idea where he stands in terms of arm strength compared to his peers; and thereby he may allow precious training time to slip by, and then one day find it's too late, as the velocity standard for him to advance to the next level is just too much for him to overcome in the time he has left.

THAT scenario is far, far less appealing to me and no less nefarious.

I wholeheartedly believe the risk of injury will always be a fact of life for high achievers in all sports. I also believe we can do specific things that would reduce that risk to acceptable levels. That track is at the essence of great coaching and development. In my opinion, restricting the use of a tool which objectively measures ball velocity doesn't seem to be a step forward.

In fact, I have found that drops in velocity measurements during a game are a terrific indicator of a fatiguing pitcher and overall a great indication of possible constraints, limitations and inefficiencies.

Velocity is...

Many professional scouts will look you right in the eye and tell you with conviction that velocity can NOT be taught. You either have it or you don't.

What they really mean to say is THEY can't teach velocity. At the Texas Baseball Ranch we develop it every single day. In all honesty, I believe it is one of the more straightforward things we do when it comes to developing the complete pitcher.

At the time I'm writing this book, since 2003 we have had 114 students top the 90 mph barrier. We have had 17 top the 95 mph barrier and two top 100. As I often joke with my clients "But who's counting?" In fact we count everything we can at The Ranch. We believe Edward Deming, the father of Quality Control, was absolutely correct when he said, "If you want to improve something, measure it!"

Our critics will snipe, "Is that off the mound or doing all that running and jumping mumbo-jumbo? Is that a peak velocity or can he sit at that velocity in a game? Sure he can throw it hard but can he throw it over 'the little white thing'? I'll bet he can't throw it that hard on a regular basis? Velo is over-rated. Give me a guy who can throw a 3-2 curveball for a strike. Aren't you worried about arm injuries if you are pushing the envelope THAT much? Sure anyone can throw it harder if you go the MAX effort route, but no one can pitch very long doing that."

I actually get a chuckle from this type of circular logic. I thought we were talking about velocity creation? If you would like to talk about command, pitchability, arm health, recovery, consistency, building a repeatable movement pattern, I'd be more than happy to so which one would you like me to discuss with you?

This sort of namby-pamby, hand wringing, mismatching critique reminds me of a person with little money turning down a far better job because he doesn't want to pay the taxes on his new significantly increased salary. Huh? That sort of thinking makes absolutely no sense to me. Having better velocity or more money isn't the be all and end all; but all things considered, it is certainly preferable to being poor or not having enough velocity.

Without question velocity can be developed and enhanced. I see it every single day. I believe one could make a very strong case that we, at The Ranch, possibly do velocity enhancement better than anyone who has ever done it before and we are far from finished evolving our processes. Not by a long shot!

What I can tell you after 20 years of doing this is that velocity creation is a multifaceted equation made up of dozens of variables. A few of those variables we cannot change. For example some of us were simply born with a higher concentration of fast twitch muscle fibers and the neuromuscular wiring to move faster than our neighbor or even our brother. However, a vast majority of those variables are within our ability to affect, enhance, augment, change, alter and/or modify.

The most frequent mistake made by parents, athletes and their coaches in my view is addressing only a few of those variables at any one time. Instead, at The Ranch we address velocity enhancement from a 360° perspective. Our goal is to affect as many of those variables positively as possible over a given time span. We refer to it as "massive simultaneous action".

Addressing only one or two of the variables often has very limited success. That is because a young man has often already developed his capacity/capability in that area about as well as he can; therefore, the potential for gain is very small.

If we use massive simultaneous action as our guiding dominant process, the chances are far greater that we will hit the area(s) with the greatest sweet spot for growth in that individual. Of course assessment is a big part of our process which enables us to tailor our training to fit each of our client's needs and his greatest potential for growth.

Summary Notes of this chapter for the Parent:

✓ Some people think of the radar gun as simply evil and believe an emphasis upon velocity creation/enhancement in youth pitchers is the very worst idea in a long line of bad ideas. Many of these people are orthopedic surgeons, physical therapists and former major league pitchers such as Tommy John.

✓ The radar gun is a tool, nothing more, nothing less. And like any other tool, it can be used for development or it can be misused and even abused and become detrimental to development. I fully believe in and utilize tools which afford me and my clients an objective measure of their progress.

✓ There are many different scenarios that can and do play out:

- ○ Players will forgo mechanical considerations, conditioning, command, movement, change of speeds and become fanatical with regards to velocity and become preoccupied in attempting to beat/top their last radar gun reading, thereby putting themselves at grave risk.

- ○ Players who are never measured by a radar gun or do not measure long toss for years might have very little idea where they stand in terms of arm strength compared to their peers and may thereby allow precious training time to slip by and then one day find it's too late, as the velocity standard to advance to the next level is just too much to overcome in the time the athlete has left.

✓ Many professional scouts will look you right in the eye and tell you with conviction that velocity can NOT be taught. "You either have it or you don't." What they really mean to say is THEY can't teach velocity. At the Texas Baseball Ranch we develop it every single day.

✓ Velocity creation is a multifaceted equation made up of dozens of variables.

✓ Your goal should be to affect as many of those variables that positively affect velocity as possible over a given time span. We refer to it as "massive simultaneous action".

Coach Wolforth's Specific Recommendations:

• Velocity = opportunity. To suggest otherwise is fallacious and/or disingenuous.

• When velocity enhancement is kept in its proper place within the model of developing the total pitching athlete, it can potentially be a real boost to someone's career.

• Find a professional instructor or a program which can guide your athlete through his personal path of velocity enhancement. There is no such thing as a one size fits all program. Stay away from those programs, as your athlete is unique and one of a kind. Sure, there will be overlap between most athletes and certainly some principles do apply to everyone; but your plan must be unique because your athlete certainly is.

Chapter 4

The Truth about Pitch Counts, Workloads and Overuse

In the past 10 years, pitch counts have become the rage.

A close personal friend of mine, Brent Strom, currently the minor league pitching coordinator for the St. Louis Cardinals, is constantly scouring through reports trying to decide, among other things, if he has assigned the appropriate workload for his minor league pitchers throughout his organization. He is a textbook case of how to utilize pitch counts effectively. He considers a myriad of variables such as age of the pitcher, arm health history, mechanical efficiency, weather, point in the season, pitch counts of the previous three starts, mental/emotional state, stressfulness/ intensity of the game (was it close or a blowout), etc.

The most common diagnosis of pitching injuries today is... drum roll please...*"overuse"*.

My personal take on these important issues:

1) Pitch counts can certainly be one of many useful tools in monitoring workloads, capacity, and shaping recovery. The trouble arises when we look at a single pitch count number (let's say 100 pitches) as a universal measurement of acceptable stress instead of an individual measurement. Every single athlete is unique. Even an individual athlete will vary significantly in his capacity from his first start in Spring Training to his last start in the World Series. For example, Nolan Ryan threw 244 pitches in a 15 inning game against the Boston Red Sox in 1971.

Many would counter:

a."But Nolan was a genetic freak!" Not so fast...The pitcher opposing Ryan that day was Luis Tiant who threw 187 pitches.

b."I bet Nolan was TOAST for the remainder of the year after that!"...Not so much. I don't believe he missed a scheduled start that year and as you already know, he had to stop pitching some 17 years later; so that outing hardly sidelined his career.

In my opinion, "pitches per inning" is a far more important factor in predicting fatigue than is simply pitches per outing. If a pitcher stays at less than 18 pitches per inning, his total pitch count is far less of a factor because he has the other half of the inning to recover. In Nolan's record night he averaged 16.2 pitches per inning. Once a pitcher goes over 25 pitches per inning, it is increasingly more difficult to fully recover prior to the next inning.

In conclusion, I believe pitch count has now unfortunately evolved into a political wedge issue—often pairing parent against coach, organization against agent and league against the local medical professional. Pitch count has often become the story in and of itself. The Washington Nationals watched Stephen Strasburg's pitch count like a hawk, yet that young man broke and needed Tommy John surgery.

Pitch count is neither bad nor good. It is simply one tool at your disposal in measuring workload. It has merit, but only, in my opinion, if it is viewed through the prism of each individual pitcher and not as this iron clad universally accepted number of acceptable/unacceptable. To view pitch count in that rigid context does far more harm than good in my opinion.

Case in point: Pitcher A throws 108 pitches in 7 innings of work. Pitcher B throws 59 pitches in 2 innings of work. Which one had, in my view, by far the more stressful night?

I would contend Pitcher B had a much tougher night because he averaged almost twice as many pitches per inning (therefore twice the workload between segments of recovery) yet threw 50 fewer pitches in total. So if we used simple pitch count totals alone in our analysis, Pitcher A had twice the workload as Pitcher B. Yet I believe when it came to stress on the soft tissue of the elbow and shoulder, one could argue the truth is exactly the opposite.

Offering a Non-baseball Analogy to Help Drive Home My Point

Pitcher A performs 15 perfect sit-ups then rests 20 minutes. He repeats the process 7 times. Pitcher B does 100 perfect sit-ups all at once without stopping. Therefore they both are at 100-105 sit-ups for that day. In other words their sit-up count is nearly exactly the same. Immediately after their 100th sit-up, let's ask each individual how stressful those 100 sit-ups were. I suggest we would get significantly different answers. Therefore I contend total pitch count is of very little true value without some very important context surrounding it. Yet many in the baseball community see it as the Holy Grail of injury reduction.

The term "Overuse" is quite frankly, in my opinion, overused. I obviously look at things from a completely different viewpoint than most medical professionals. I see most injuries not so much as overuse as cases of athletes being under-prepared for the specific stress they are about to encounter at game time.

Here is why I say that. Today, if I went out and tried to run 26 miles and got hurt, was that "overuse" or "under-preparation"? It would be impossible for anyone to correctly answer that question unless you were privy to my complete training process for the past 6 months.

Nolan Ryan could throw 244 pitches in a single outing because his preparation and his high level of mechanical efficiency allowed him to extend his skill specific endurance to levels most couldn't touch. I contend "overuse" is a blanket diagnosis which medical professionals hide behind to attempt to explain the unexplainable i.e. exactly why did Johnny get hurt.

For these reasons, I am very skeptical on most uses/applications of pitch counts and the all too common diagnosis of "overuse".

★ Personal Note to Parent:

If after reading this chapter, it is clear that this subject is one of your athlete's constraints or limitations and you would like to go into deeper detail, you need to check out our "Accelerated Arm Recovery" program. I teamed up with Lee Fiochi of Dynamic Sports Training to put together this program. Everyone wants to know what to do after pitching in a game. Well, now there's an answer. **On this 77 minute DVD, you will be taken through specific steps to improve recovery as much as 300%.**

Go to PitchingCentral.com and search "Arm Recovery"

Summary Notes of this Chapter for the Parent:

- ✓ The term "overuse" is overused.
- ✓ The trouble arises when we look at a single pitch count number (let's say 100 pitches) as a *universal* measurement of acceptable stress instead of an *individual* measurement.
- ✓ Pitches per inning are a far more important factor in predicting fatigue than is pitches per outing. If a pitcher throws less than 18 pitches per inning, his total pitch count is far less of a factor because he has the other half of the inning to recover.
- ✓ I believe pitch count has now unfortunately evolved into a political wedge issue—often pairing parent against coach, organization against agent and league against the local medical professional. Pitch count has often become the story in and of itself.
- ✓ There is a big difference between "under prepared" and "overuse". A vast majority of pitchers are under prepared. Which one are you?

Coach Wolforth's Specific Recommendations:

- Pitch count is a valid method of assessing and tracking workloads. Just because pitch counts are often over-simplified and/or misapplied by the general baseball culture doesn't mean they DON'T have merit. Pitch count as a general tool for monitoring workload is absolutely fine. It's the over-generalized way it is typically utilized with which I have an issue.

- "Pitches per inning" is a more important measurement of workload in my view, as innings exceeding 25 pitches are far more stressful than innings using less than 15 pitches. In essence, the total pitch count is less important than the way you get there. Spacing 120 pitches over 9 innings is a far less stressful day than is 80 pitches over 3 innings.

- My advice is to pay attention to both total pitch count and pitch count per inning. Start the preseason with a low pitch count of 30 pitches in your athlete's first outing and incrementally increase that work load over time—based upon how the athlete responds and feels.

- Pitch count per inning should always be watched carefully and a vast majority of pitchers should never extend their night further after one inning of 35, two innings of 30 or three innings of 25.

- Personally I don't believe in "overuse". Instead I believe injury occurs when the specific demands, intensity and/or duration exceed the amount of preparation. Most athletes are underprepared and not overused.

Chapter 5

The Truth about "Mechanics"

Let's begin our discussion on mechanics with a simple quiz just to establish your personal level of competence on the topic of "pitching mechanics". Which of these exhibits…A, B, C or D, in your opinion, represents the best or most sound mechanics of the four pictures in the group? Take your time and rate them best to worst. We shall see just how competent you are as an evaluator of mechanical efficiency.

Exhibits A-D

On the next page are the results.

And the correct answer is:

They ALL are of Roger Clemens at different phases of his delivery

A reminder to us all that no matter how intelligent we think we are or how well we think we understand a subject, we all look at things through a biased lens. I believe each of us must work hard at remaining very humble when it comes to dissecting something as complex as human movement patterns.

We all have our pet movements and positions and if we aren't careful they can blind us from seeing the big picture. How we phrase the question or approach the question very well may BE the problem. As that "great pitching coach" Albert Einstein once said, "Make everything as simple as possible but not simpler."

The next question I have for those who talk about "mechanics" as if it were one monolithic, universal, ideal model in which all the experts agree: "EXACTLY whose mechanics are you talking about anyway?"

Bob Feller's Mechanics or Roger Clemens Mechanics?

Sandy Koufax's mechanics or Randy Johnson's?

Pedro Martinez's mechanics or Juan Marichal's?

Even Cliff Lee's mechanics or Roy Halladay's?

Because… "This just in"…ALL these guys were/are pretty good OVER a LONG time.

The truth is no two pitchers in the history of baseball have EVER thrown identically. Therefore from our vantage point at The Texas Baseball Ranch, insisting that there is one ideal mechanical model, or in other words, "cookie cutting" or "cloning" your pitchers is one of the very worst things one could do to a young man. Yet we see this scene play out again and again, every single day, all over the world.

The "Cookie Cutter" Model: Standard operating procedure for a vast majority of baseball environments.

And it is almost ALWAYS done with love and the very best of intentions.

My sincere advice: Stay away from anyone who wants to place your athlete inside of a specific mold. However well intended, it almost always ends poorly.

No matter where you live in the year 2013, because of the World Wide Web, you can find the exact information you need to help your athlete approach his/her God-given potential. Don't surrender or acquiesce responsibility to someone who doesn't understand the innate uniqueness of your son simply because that instructor played some professional baseball or because a training facility is located very conveniently to your home and for your schedule. In my opinion, we owe our children better than that. We owe it to them to get them the very best information we possibly can.

Bottom line: I urge you to look at pitching mechanics from a decidedly different perspective. If your instructor or coach doesn't understand or utilize at the very least 50% of the following phrases/concepts, I would keep searching until I found one that did and can, at minimum, supplement your training at home:

Holistic Training/Skill specific Training
Synchronization/Sequencing
Mobility/Stability
Posture/Rotation/Connection
Guided Discovery/Natural Learning
Rhythm/Timing/Tempo/Intent
Deceleration/Pronation/Scapular stabilization
Periodization/Accommodation/Training effect
Individualism / Degrees of Freedom
Muscle fiber type recruitment/Energy Systems/Recovery

Personal Note to Parent:

The "Connection" concept and training is <u>the most significant distinction</u> made at Pitching Central & Ron Wolforth's Texas Baseball Ranch since 2003.

This distinction has already helped hundreds of pitchers significantly reduce, and in most cases eliminate, any arm issues. If after reading this chapter, it is clear that this subject is one of your athlete's primary constraints or limitations and you would like to go into deeper detail, you'll want to check out **the "Connection" DVD which takes you through this critical but overlooked link to improved pitching performance.**

Go to <u>PitchingCentral.com</u> and search "Connection"

Summary Notes of this Chapter for the Parent:

✓ No matter how intelligent we think we are or how well we think we understand a subject, we all look at things through a biased lens. I believe each of us must work hard at remaining very humble when it comes to dissecting something as complex as human movement patterns.

✓ The question I have for those who talk about "mechanics" as if it were one monolithic, universal, ideal model in which all the experts agree: EXACTLY whose "mechanics" are you talking about being ideal anyway?

✓ The truth is no two pitchers in the history of baseball have EVER thrown identically. Therefore from our vantage point at the Texas Baseball Ranch, insisting that there is one ideal mechanical model, or in other words, "cookie cutting" or "cloning" your pitchers, is one of the very worst things one could do to a young man.

✓ My sincere advice: Stay away from anyone who wants to place you inside of a specific mold. However well intended, it almost always ends poorly.

✓ Don't surrender or acquiesce responsibility to someone who doesn't understand the innate uniqueness of your son simply because that instructor played some professional baseball or because a training facility is located very conveniently to your home and for your schedule.

✓ Protect your athlete by understanding his movement patterns better than anyone else.

Coach Wolforth's Specific Recommendations:

- The term "mechanics" is one of the most overused and clichéd terms in all of baseball. It has morphed into a nebulous set of descriptions in which rarely more than two people are in full agreement. I simply do not use the term. I avoid its use intentionally. In its stead I use the term "mechanical efficiencies" rather than "mechanics". "Mechanical efficiencies" implies the efficiency of **movement**. "Mechanics" implies specific body part **positioning** in space. At the Texas Baseball Ranch, we are far more concerned with movement than we are with a particular body part position in space and time.

- At the Texas Baseball Ranch we assign each student to a model who has similar styles and movement characteristics. This model is a successful pitcher who had a long, distinguished career **AND** was healthy.

- I strongly urge you to reject the concept of "One Universal Ideal Mechanical Model". In my opinion, such a model doesn't exist and insisting that one does is commonly a major contributor to many athletes' stagnation and/or underachievement.

Chapter 6

The Truth about Long Toss

The internet is replete with thousands of ideas and opinions on the efficacy of long toss for pitchers. Some coaches and gurus contend long toss is one of the most dangerous activities a pitcher could possibly engage in from a health and injury perspective. Others claim it's simply a waste of valuable training time because it doesn't follow the principle of specificity and confuses release points and encourages inefficient game time mound mechanics. Still others insinuate it's a Godsend and is the answer to almost any pitching ailment with which your athlete could possibly be confronted.

The result is that many parents and coaches get frozen by this myriad of wide swinging opinions. They don't want to hurt their young man or place him in unnecessary risk; yet on the other hand they know how closely tied having a power/ electric arm is to opportunity and advancement; so they often become frozen with indecision and choose a middle course which all but guarantees mediocrity.

A few internet gurus even claim they have a specific recipe which overrides or shortcuts the long toss route. To me personally, most of these recipes are simply attempts at marketing their product, attempts at simply being provocative for effect and/or are a flat out "red herring".

So where does The Ranch fall on the long toss continuum?

The answer is WAY, WAY toward the "long toss is a Godsend and the answer" end of the spectrum. While we don't quite view long toss as the ultimate answer for EVERY aliment; long toss, in our view, is an exceptionally valuable instrument in our tool box for developing the powerful/electric arm.

For those who knock long toss as a valuable asset in one's development toolbox (and in fact they are many, including many in professional baseball), I find they most often fail to grasp, recognize or accept two primary truths.

Truth #1. One can throw without pitching, but one can never pitch without throwing, meaning clearly that throwing begets pitching, not the other way around. Therefore to become a prolific pitcher, one must first become a prolific thrower. This truth is simply not debatable.

Truth #2. There are two primary elements involved in being a world class pitcher. One is skill. The other is ability. You will need both. Long toss is an ability creator/augmenter/enhancer/developer. The body is forced by its goal of maximum distance to organize itself differently and recruit body parts/potential contributors differently. This assists us in creating the training effect we often seek.

Neither one of these truths is insignificant.

I personally find those who rail against long toss are often obsessed or stuck on the skill side of the equation and simply can't see that it will be in the freedom, the experimentation, the self-discovery, the expansion and the body's organization for length where multiple benefits of skill specific strength, range of

Nikolai Bernstein proving his Theorem of "degrees of freedom" in even repetitive movements.

motion, neuromuscular firing, accommodation and recruitment can and will take place.

Motor Learning Pioneer Russian Nikolai Bernstein, the man responsible for coining the term *"biomechanics"*, had a hypothesis (later referred to by engineer Paul Nyman as the **Bernstein Principle**) that we use as the core of our training at The Ranch.

The Bernstein Principle: *The body will organize itself based upon the ultimate goal of the activity.*

In other words, if the brain's goal is for the body to throw the ball for maximum distance or maximum speed, the body will then organize itself to achieve that goal. In essence the goal or intent of the activity directly affects how the body responds.

This is specifically why long toss, in my opinion, is a very beneficial activity. It encourages the body to recruit and organize itself for higher end point velocities. Does THAT sound like a good idea to you? Yes or no?

Let me close this chapter with a story I often tell at clinics or when I'm consulting to make my point on the efficacy of long toss vs. all the naysayers out there who literally pick the activity to death.

The anti-long toss people's primary criticism of long toss can most often be boiled down to the fact that it is not game-like enough and actually interferes with the "ideal mechanics and release points" needed to pitch a baseball at the highest levels. In their opinion, the only way a pitcher can develop into a high caliber pitcher is to actually pitch off a mound at game distance.

I counter this argument by taking them precisely at their point.

Let me explain.

Imagine we have two identical twins. At age 3 we begin to let them throw. Twin A, we'll refer to as the Freedom Twin. Twin B, we'll refer to as the Specificity Twin.

Twin A, we encourage and allow to move back as far as he can every single session he throws. In essence we will allow him to throw long toss every time out. We measure his distance and the next time he throws we encourage him to see if he can exceed his distance from his last time out. The only stipulation we place on him is that he cannot back up until he can hit his partner 10 consecutive times without his partner moving more than 1 step in any direction.

Twin B on the other hand, we limit to never going further back and throwing even one foot further than he would actually pitch in a game at his age level. So up until he is 12, Twin B never throws a ball beyond 46 feet and spends his time focusing exclusively on mechanics. By the time he reaches 14 years of age, the specificity twin is working primarily off a mound 60'6" away. So from the age of 3 until he is 18, Twin B has NEVER thrown a ball more than 60' 6" away from his target...and I repeat never, under any circumstances will the specificity twin be allowed to throw a ball beyond 60'6".

From the age of 3 until they are both 18, these two boys throw three times a week, 40 weeks of the year for about 45 minutes a session. They throw the same exact number of throws. The only difference is in their process.

You tell me which twin has the strongest and most powerful arm?

You see the anti-long toss people would scoff at the 60'6" limitation as ridiculous, but I'm just forcing them to strictly adhere to their stated principles. If specificity is indeed the be all and end all of pitching, I'm simply not allowing them to have it both ways. From my perspective, most of these self-proclaimed experts obviously fail to recognize the difference between skill and ability.

Elite performers certainly do need high levels of skill—no question. But they also need exceptionally high levels of ability as well. And just like any other animal in nature, if constrained to a much smaller space than is ideal, they can never and will never grow and expand to the limits of their natural ability.

I will state for the record that long toss is not a panacea. It does not cure all pitching ailments. Long toss is simply a tool. It certainly can be misused, misapplied, mishandled, have an improper emphasis or be improperly executed or administered. All that said, the risk of utilizing long toss pales in consequence to failing to use it as part of your total development package. In my opinion, long toss is an absolutely invaluable tool for any aspiring young pitcher.

Personal Note to Parent:

The Texas Baseball Ranch and Pitching Central have a very specific Long Toss regimen. If after reading this chapter, it is clear that this subject is one of your athlete's primary constraints or limitations and you would like to go into deeper detail, **Coach Wolforth has created a DVD that answers key questions including the philosophy behind long toss, countering critics, the actual process/method as well as the frequency at different stages in the season.**

Go To PitchingCentral.com and search "Long Toss"

Summary Notes of this Chapter for the Parent:

Parents and coaches get frozen by the myriad of wide swinging opinions on the subject of long toss and lose the opportunity for growth that correctly administered long toss can afford.

- ✓ The Texas Baseball Ranch views long toss as a valuable tool for developing a powerful and electric arm.
- ✓ One can throw without pitching, but one can never pitch without throwing. To become a prolific pitcher, one must first become a prolific thrower. Elite performers need high levels of both skill and ability. Long Toss is an ability creator/ augmenter/enhancer/developer.

✓ The Bernstein Principle: The body will organize itself based on the ultimate goal of the activity. Therefore if the brain's goal is for the body to throw the ball maximum distance or maximum speed, the body will then organize itself to achieve that goal.

✓ Long Toss is very beneficial because it encourages the body to recruit and organize itself for higher end point velocities.

✓ Long Toss is not a panacea. It can be misused, misapplied, mishandled, have an improper emphasis or be improperly executed or administered.

✓ The risk of utilizing long toss pales in consequence to failing to use it as part of any player's total development program.

Coach Wolforth's Specific Recommendations:

• Research long toss on your own and develop your own personal philosophy. Don't leave it up to some guru to tell you what you should believe. You personally craft and mold long toss to fit your individual athlete's specific needs.

• Long toss, while not a panacea and only as effective as the athlete's process, is a very valuable tool in your total development program.

Chapter 7

The Truth about Weighted Balls

Of the four topics most frequently debated on internet pitching forums and blogs—curveballs, pitch counts, long toss and weighted balls—I find the debate on weighted balls the most intriguing and the most commonly misunderstood by the general baseball population at large.

Twenty years ago I was very averse to long toss and weighted ball training. Now in 2013, I would be considered possibly one of the world's strongest advocates for both. So what changed my perspective on the utilization of weighted balls?

The first thing that changed for me was the realization that a baseball is itself indeed a "weighted ball". It weighs just over 5 ounces. So many people have the myopic view that a baseball is a 100% safe weight and another ball of a greater weight must therefore automatically be more dangerous.

This is simply on its face an untrue, faulty and in my opinion, a very limiting assumption.

A regulation 12" softball weighs just over 6 ounces in weight. A regulation football weighs 15 ounces. So if the simple weight of the ball was directly related to its risk of generating injury, softball throwers would show a slightly greater propensity for injury than baseball throwers and football quarterbacks would roughly be at three times the risk of injury as that of baseball players. Yet the exact opposite is actually true.

Paul Nyman actually asserts if a baseball happened to weigh 7 ounces instead of 5, we'd see FEWER injuries, not more. I concur.

53

So how do we reconcile the conventional wisdom with the actual truth?

This task has been made more difficult because there are some gurus and those in professional baseball that have taken a very high profile position in which they have been publicly outspoken against the utilization of "weighted" balls. For many, taking such an adamant position at one point proves very difficult to walk back.

Now, in all fairness, several anti-weighted ball folks would counter, "But you don't throw a football like you throw a baseball." Duly noted. That is a totally separate issue, but the key point I don't want you to miss is that adding weight to a ball does not automatically add risk to the throw. In fact, I personally have experienced the opposite. Let me walk you through this process.

#1. The lighter the ball we utilize, the higher the potential end point velocity that can be created.

#2. The higher the end point velocity, the more efficient the acceleration and deceleration of the arm must be to avoid injury.

#3. The higher the end point velocity, the greater potential stress to soft tissue.

In essence I'm saying a 2 ounce wiffle ball thrown at full speed is potentially more risky than throwing a water logged 8 ounce baseball at full speed.

Track and field coaches have experimented with overload and under-load training for decades. From a sport dealing with fractions of seconds and fractions of inches separating greatness and fame from abject obscurity, baseball certainly could learn a few things.

Baseball on the other hand is a game of nuance and skill where a strike out pitch thrown 105 mph counts exactly the same as a strike out pitch thrown at 65 mph...and a home run hit 459 feet counts exactly as much as one hit 301 feet. This makes creating exceptional baseball results far more obscure and murky than simply improving a long jumper's distance or reducing a sprinter's time.

I personally believe this complexity regarding creating better baseball outcomes is the primary reason people fail to appreciate the role weighted balls can play in the training process. If, for example, long distance throwing or improving a radar reading were sports in and of themselves, I wholeheartedly believe the baseball culture at large would view weighted balls much differently.

I contend the resistance to utilizing this tool is founded primarily in the area we discussed in the previous chapter, which is the confusion between pitching skill and throwing ability.

Developing the skill to throw a 5 oz. ball to a spot 60' 6" away is a decidedly different goal than developing the ability to throw a 5 oz. ball 100 mph or 380 feet.

Ironically there are actually a few things my detractors and I agree on: One being, as I mentioned last chapter, that we both agree that it will indeed take a high level of BOTH skill and ability to perform well at the highest levels of competition. However, where we part ways is in our beliefs in how skill and ability are created, augmented, enhanced, improved and ultimately developed.

So How do we Utilize Weighted Balls at The Ranch? Where do Weighted Balls Fit into our Training Process?

Weighted balls are used at The Ranch primarily for arm care and warm-up. We use them every single day. They are a staple of our preparation. We began experimenting with weighted balls in 2002 in an effort to improve velocity; but we have found that while they did help some in that regard, their greatest contribution was that of improving health and durability.

We don't EVER "pitch" a ball other than the 5 ¼ oz. game ball. Pitching a baseball is a skill. When we pitch, we use a regulation baseball. However we do throw balls as heavy as 6 lbs., all the way down to 3.5 ounces into our target pad from 8-30 feet away...depending upon the weight of the ball and the drill we use. For the heavier balls, 2-6 lbs., we use a very specific movement pattern and are much closer (8-15 feet) to the target pad.

We do not long toss with weighted balls, although I'm not necessarily opposed to the basic concept; I just think the specific weights need to be addressed individually and we have not experimented enough in this area to give quality advice. So as of the writing of this book in 2013, we at The Ranch do not use weighted balls in our long toss progressions.

Bottom line: Like long toss, we view weighted balls simply as a tool. Weighted balls certainly can be misused, misapplied, mishandled, have an improper emphasis or be improperly executed or administered. All that said, the risk of utilizing weighted balls pales in consequence to failing to use them as part of your total development package. In my opinion, if used effectively, weighted balls can be an absolutely invaluable tool for any aspiring young pitcher.

Personal Note to Parent:

Deceleration is a much-overlooked topic and I believe it is "Ground Zero" for pitchers and their movement patterns. If after reading this chapter, it is clear that this subject is one of your athlete's primary constraints or limitations and you would like to go into deeper detail, I have created a 64 minute DVD just on this topic and **I believe it is a MUST for every pitcher who is looking to have a long, healthy & durable career.**

Go To PitchingCentral.com and search "Deceleration"

Summary Notes of this Chapter for the Parent:

✓ Weighted ball use is one of the most commonly misunderstood topics by the baseball population at large.

✓ A baseball is a "weighted ball"—just over 5 ounces.

✓ If ball weight was related to injury risk, softball throwers would show a greater propensity for injury than baseball; football quarterbacks would be at three times the risk.

✓ A case for lighter weights actually being more dangerous:

  o The lighter the ball, the higher potential end point velocity.

  o The higher the end point velocity, the more efficient acceleration and deceleration must be to avoid injury.

  o The higher the end point velocity, the greater potential for stress to soft tissue.

✓ People fail to appreciate the role of weighted balls in the training process due to the complexity regarding creating better baseball outcomes.

✓ Resistance to using weighted balls is primarily due to confusion between "pitching skill" and "throwing ability" (See Chapter 6).

✓ At the Texas Baseball Ranch, weighted balls are used primarily for arm care and warm-up.

✓ Weighted balls have contributed greatly to improving arm health and durability.

Coach Wolforth's Specific Recommendations:

• Never "pitch" a ball other than a regulation baseball.

• Balls up to 6 lbs. all the way down to 3.5 oz. can be thrown into the target pad (www.thepitchingpad.com) from 8-30 ft. depending on the weight of the ball and the drill used.

• Weighted balls are not currently recommended as of this writing (2013) to be used in long toss.

• View weighted balls as one of many tools in your development program tool box.

Chapter 8

The Truth about Command/Control

While developing velocity and keeping pitchers healthy are very often complex and sometimes even multitudinous endeavors, developing command is not.

As the old yarn goes, "This is actually very simple but it sure isn't easy."

Command is predominantly about developing a repeatable movement pattern. One builds a repeatable movement pattern ONLY by good old-fashion deliberate practice and lots of it.

Command, control or accuracy are not techniques. Many in baseball would have you believe that you can only have command with "good mechanics". First of all, the central paradigm is flawed. Second, even if the paradigm wasn't fatally flawed, the truth is no two people could agree completely on what constitutes good mechanics. I believe after you see the following two examples you will see why narrowing down human movement patterns into an "ideal" movement model is not an exact science—to say the least. Personally I believe it to be a waste of time.

Let me give you two examples which will prove my point about developing command beyond a reasonable doubt.

Example #1

Example #2

A sport which has an even greater emphasis placed upon control than baseball would be golf. So how do we explain how three of the greatest golfers of all time, Arnold Palmer, Lee Trevino and Jim Furyk have become top performers? Their movement patterns are clearly FAR from having the classic golf swings of Ben Hogan, Byron Nelson or Jack Nicholas.

The answer is thousands and thousands of hours of practice and a ridiculous amount of time banging range balls and shaping their craft. Through repetition and hours of trial and error (remember the Bernstein Principle) they developed a pattern that worked. It wasn't necessarily "pretty" or "classic" but it was effective.

Juan Marichal and Dan Quisenberry are two of the all-time best in MLB history with regards to giving up the fewest walks per 9 innings. In other words, their control/accuracy or command is considered among the greatest of all time. Yet, neither one of them is anywhere close to what would be considered by most in baseball as having classic or textbook mechanics. Furthermore if you look closely, they are both right handed and are not only far from classic, they are almost opposites of each other.

So how do we explain how two of the greatest control pitchers of all time were so successful even though their movement patterns were so FAR from what the conventional model of "ideal" is considered to be?

The answer is thousands and thousands of hours of deliberate practice and a ridiculous amount of time throwing balls and shaping their craft (the Bernstein Principle again). Through repetition and hours of trial and error they developed a pattern that worked. It wasn't necessarily pretty but it was effective.

Bottom line:

Practice, practice, and practice your technique.

Control/Accuracy/Command are developed almost exclusively by deliberate practice.

Control/Accuracy/Command are NOT techniques or positions in space and time.

Everyone talks about having a repeatable delivery, but I remind everyone the word "repeat" is a verb, not a noun. Therefore "repeatability" is a process, not a thing or a yes or no answer.

I suggest therefore that what we are in fact seeking is a mechanically efficient movement pattern and then training that pattern so our delivery is more and more repeatable.

So in essence, once we find a pattern that works, then we have to go to work—just like former greats Palmer, Trevino, Furyk, Marichal and Quisenberry.

★ **Personal Note to Parent:**

At The Texas Baseball Ranch and Pitching Central, we have a very unique insight into improving and mastering command both for your fastball and off-speed pitches. If after reading this chapter, it is clear that this subject is one of your athlete's primary constraints or limitations and you would like to go into deeper detail, I have put together a 126 minute training DVD designed to help the beginner pitcher and challenge the advanced pitcher. **It takes a look at many of the common mistakes most people make when training command.**

Go To PitchingCentral.com and search "Command"

Summary Notes of this Chapter for the Parent:

- ✓ Command is predominantly about developing a repeatable movement pattern.
- ✓ One builds a repeatable movement pattern ONLY by a lot of deliberate practice.
- ✓ Command, control or accuracy is NOT a technique or "good mechanics".
- ✓ Juan Marichal and Dan Quisenberry are two of the all-time best in MLB history with regard to giving up the fewest walks per 9 innings (equal to having good command) yet neither of them is close to what most in baseball consider having classic or textbook mechanics.

Chapter 9

The Truth about Wake-up, Warm-up

One of the most frequent mistakes made by pitchers today, in my opinion, is that they are significantly underprepared for the volume (total workload) and/or the intensity of the stress placed by pitching at the highest levels of competition. I'll discuss the specifics regarding the preparation for the volume/workload of elite competition in **Chapter 10, *The Truth about the Conditioning of Pitchers***. In this chapter, I'm going to discuss the truth with regards to preparing your pitcher for the intensity of elite competition.

If there is one truism about us as human beings, it is that we often secretly hope the job, any job, won't be quite so arduous, complex or difficult as we know deep in our subconscious that it probably will be.

Case in point: Millions of weekend golfers hit the links every Saturday and Sunday. Their process: 1) Arrive an hour before scheduled tee time. 2) A quick stop in the pro shop for tees, balls or a new glove or visor. 3) Pick up the golf cart. 4) Drive to the range and do a light stretch using a club. 5) Hit a medium bucket of range balls, primarily emphasizing the driver and short irons. 6) Make a quick stop at the putting green for 10-15 putts. 7) Then it's off to the first tee. 8) By the turn, our frustration and our use of colorful language are well oiled machines. 9) By the 18th hole, we've struggled mightily but have hit enough decent shots to convince ourselves that with a professional lesson or two, a new wedge/putter and/or a better attitude/focus, next Saturday we can actually break (100, 90, 80, 75).

As my father used to say, "Denial is not a river in Africa."

And how exactly is that process going for us? For millions of weekend golfers, in truth, not well at all. In fact I contend that it's a process actually guaranteeing mediocrity.

But that's the golf weekend "wanna be", right?

Well, traditional baseball warm-ups are in truth not even 5% better. See if you recognize this process.

1) The players arrive one hour prior to the game.
2) The players run a lap or run to centerfield and back.
3) The players circle up and perform a casual stretch.
4) The players then play catch to warm up, primarily backing up to 90 to 120 feet away.
5) The players then come in and take a quick infield and then some dry swings or cuts off a tee.
6) For ELITE teams, the team has a quick live BP.
7) 45 minutes prior to a game the pitcher also does a light stretch/tubing; then at the 30 minute mark he lightly tosses until the catcher backs up to about 120 feet or so. At 15 minutes until game time, the pitcher throws a 20-30 pitch bull pen, then grabs his jacket, gets a drink of water and sits down in the dugout. He's obviously ready to go "blow em' up!"

How quaint. Taking poetic license from an old TV commercial, "There is *ready to go*!...then there is ....*Not exactly.*" I contend for a vast majority of pitchers it's "*not exactly*" that describes their preparation.

Does ANY part of that process I describe strike you as preparing yourself exceptionally well for throwing 100 mph or absolutely being ready for PEAK performance and dominating the first hitters you face?

For example, if I knew later today I was going to run 100 meters for a GOLD medal which would establish me as the best sprinter in the world today, would I prepare for that race in the same manner?

I think the answer is obvious.

I have a saying that I use often with my clients at The Ranch. "Your body can't possibly recruit what isn't awake." My inference being that if parts of your body are not fully awake, lubricated and ready to be utilized, they simply will not be available for use.

Throwing a baseball 70 mph at 12 years of age or 80 mph at 14, 85 at 16, 90 at 18 or 95 at 22 will almost always require the FULL utilization of ALL of our body, not just our arm. Yet I have found that most athletes HOPE they can perform at peak levels with less than FULL utilization/wake-up/warm-up of their body. It is an act of delusion. But it's actually much more than that. It is dangerous.

Everyone, even the least baseball savvy of parents, conceptually understands that to throw hard requires far more than just their son's arm. Yet, very few people at ALL levels of baseball give attention to the critical importance of the entire body being fully and completely awake and lathered.

A pitcher having to rely primarily on his arm for peak velocity and performance is placed at even greater risk of injury than otherwise would be the case.

At The Ranch we view wake-up/warm-up as absolutely critical to success. It is one of those things in which we have zero tolerance. EVERY single pitcher could be completely warmed up before he goes in, but very, very few are. It is simply a choice.

What would you venture to guess is the number one excuse as to why being fully warmed-up doesn't happen very often?

By far, the most common fear, both conscious and unconscious, is the fear that if their warm-up is too extensive they will be too fatigued or worn out to last the entire game.

My response:

They way you view the problem may very well be the problem.

If you are too worn out from the warm-up and then have a drop in performance at game time, your warm-up may not be your primary issue. You may instead have a CONDITIONING issue. That one is easy to solve.

Always keep in mind, the warm-up is as individual as the pitcher himself and should be evolving and growing just like he is. There is, of course, no one ideal warm-up process. Dedicate yourself to finding the right level of personal readiness for peak performance. One practical gauge I suggest is that if you tend to struggle in the first inning, you need to ramp up your warm-up to the point that you feel you are in what we refer to at The Ranch as "a 3rd inning lather".

If you would make a habit of warming up in that manner, your body would soon not only adjust to the warm-up but actually CRAVE that kind of stimulation and readiness.

On the other hand, if you tend to start very strong but fade in the 3rd and 4th inning you might want to look at BOTH your warm-up AND your conditioning. You might want to pull back on the intensity and duration of your warm-up AND work a little harder on your conditioning.

If you need a warm-up role model at the elite level to follow, study past greats like Nolan Ryan, Roger Clemens or current star Roy Halladay. My long time student Trevor Bauer has meticulously developed his pregame preparation over the past 6 years and the core of his wake-up/warm-up can be found in the New Athletic Pitcher Program. While others are constantly berating and criticizing Trevor for his lengthy and involved wake-up/warm-up process, they often miss the fact that he designed it personally to fit his own specific needs, personality and proclivities. In other words, it works for him.

Of the dozens of Ranch pitchers that are competing at the collegiate and professional levels, no two have the exact same warm-up. Each athlete is encouraged and taught to continually develop one that will work for him individually.

They are also encouraged to create 3 different wake-up/ warm-ups.

1. **Their ideal warm-up with no time constraints (We refer to this as Wake-up/Warm-up A)**
2. **A shortened version of their ideal wake-up/warm-up in which they can be ready in 25 minutes (We refer to this as Wake-up/Warm-up B)**
3. **An emergency version in which they make the absolute most out of a 12-15 minute window (We refer to this as Wake-up/Warm-up C)**

This exercise can be very valuable to the pitcher as their roles or their situations change. In other words they could become an emergency starter due to a last minute sickness or an injury, deal with rain delays, a breakdown of the team bus or be moved into the bull pen. Having all 3 processes in your back pocket is a very valuable thing indeed.

 I've prepared something very special for my readers that will assist you in continuing your elite pitcher experience. Download Your Free Report:

"Why 95% of Pitchers Fail and How You Can Avoid Being One of Them"
At: www.TexasBaseballRanch.com

Summary Notes of this Chapter for the Parent:

✓ One of the most frequent mistakes most pitchers make is being significantly underprepared for the volume and/or intensity of the stress of pitching at the highest levels of competition.

✓ Everyone conceptually understands throwing hard requires more than just the use of the arm; yet few give it the appropriate attention.

✓ At the Texas Baseball Ranch there is zero tolerance for lack of an efficient warm-up.

✓ A pitcher's number one excuse for not being fully warmed-up is fear of fatigue. This is not a warm-up issue; it's a conditioning issue.

✓ Good warm-up models are Nolan Ryan, Roger Clemens, Roy Halladay and Trevor Bauer.

Chapter 10

The Truth about the Conditioning of Pitchers

This chapter represents a great passion for me personally. In developing my understanding of the very best ways to condition my clients for elite competition, I have had the honor of listening to and learning from some of the best minds in the sports performance industry.

There is absolutely no reason why, with some degree of earnest work, the average person cannot become very familiar with incredible training protocols which would truly assist their son or daughter who is an elite athlete. I would suggest starting with the following 6 names: Eric Cressey, Dr. Charlie Weingroff, Michael Boyle, Vern Gambetta, Lee Fiocchi and Gray Cook. These men will provide an incredible foundation and will probably lead you on to others. Bottom line, there is no shortage of very intelligent people who will give you great direction for your athlete in his or her development from a skill specific strength and conditioning standpoint.

For me personally, my formal education began in Pre-Medicine. Later in my academic career, I changed my major to Kinesiology so this path of literally chasing sports performance has in fact been a very natural one for me. My postgraduate work further involved Physical Education and Motor Learning. Of course this path has been extremely beneficial for me in my present profession. But for me, the most significant thing which influenced my current understanding and clarity started almost ten years ago with reading a training manual by Dr. Mel Siff, entitled *Supertraining*. In his work he discusses the Russian model of training which distinguishes GPP (General Physical Preparedness) with SPP (Specific Physical Preparedness). Dr. Siff's work really resonated with me and continues to influence my path today at The Ranch.

In short, the Russians understood that not all training was identical or, more importantly, appropriate for every athlete. For our training to have maximum benefit, we as the trainer must match the appropriate training to the appropriate athlete as well as fit the training to each athlete based upon his/her personal level of readiness and the specific point in his competitive season. Of course that would require assessment. Unfortunately the terms "physical assessment" or "level of preparedness" and "baseball training" usually do not coexist closely together. I assure you they do at The Ranch.

It is true that almost every player at any level will get a "physical" from medical professionals, but that assessment is certainly far from determining GPP.

At the professional and college level, the baseball people typically roll their eyes while the strength and athletic training staff perform their obligatory assessments when the players first report. The baseball people then have to wait patiently, until finally, they get their turn and they feel the real work can begin. It's a sad paradigm really.

The reality that we ALL need to come to grips with is that if ANY training is below an individual athlete's level of preparedness, you in fact have wasted much of their time. If, on the other hand, the training is significantly above their level of preparedness, you have placed them at increased risk of injury. I see this circumstance almost every single day and it is quite frankly, in my opinion, inexcusable.

71

I have attended Spring Trainings for seven years straight and I've often maintained, based on what I've witnessed, the best way my professional clients could prepare for Spring Training is to spend a week at Disney standing in line for hours waiting for their 30 seconds bouts of hyperactivity. It would be humorous if it weren't so true.

Baseball is a game of "uber-tradition". Much of Spring Training hasn't changed since the 1950's. Some of the tradition is wonderful, endearing and productive. Some of it is simply getting in the way of the natural evolution of baseball training.

It will take some owner to become **completely** fed up with the exorbitant funds spent on workman's compensation, coupled with the large amount of time lost on the disabled list, to begin to hold feet to the fire. THEN things will begin to change.

Today, most owners and GMs have a genuine reverence toward those ex-major leaguers now in charge of running the game and still tend to acquiesce to the knowledge and experience of the baseball veterans. They don't want to rock the boat too much. It's understandable on an emotional level. Experience is without question important and valuable but so is research and development. New ideas being infused into baseball's lifeblood is absolutely critical for its growth.

As an important aside, many athletes now have personal trainers and get their assessments individually, so the game has evolved in that way over the past 20 years. The downside to that dynamic is often the organization, that yearns for some modicum of control over a critically important contributor and high price commodity, is often placed at direct opposition to the personal trainers who work hard for influence over the same athlete. Two famous cases would be Roger Clemens and his personal trainer, Brian McNamee and Barry Bonds and his personal trainer, Greg Anderson.

It is an imperfect dynamic for sure. This scenario has been made much worse in my opinion because baseball hasn't kept up with or applied much of the latest advancements in training.

Currently a vast majority of the "baseball people" in the organization are, for the most part, disengaged from the strength, athletic training and physical therapy side and find their work basically anything from a necessary evil to a real pain in the backside. Often the two groups actually view each other with quiet and hidden contempt.

With all that said, let me cut to the chase and tell you what you as a parent need to know about the conditioning of your pitcher

#1. Assessment. Regardless if your athlete is 9 or 29 years of age, before beginning his conditioning I believe you must find a high caliber physical therapist for an assessment. I strongly recommend finding a PT who is certified to perform a Functional Movement Screening. However, if one of those is not available in your area, still seek out a Physical Therapist who works regularly with elite athletes and get a physical assessment.

You as a parent want to know where your athlete may have possible constraints, limitations or restrictions. How is his flexibility and mobility? How is his structural alignment and strength balance? How is his strength and stability? The last thing you want to do is build strength over dysfunction or add mobility to something already hyper-mobile.

Then after the assessment, politely but firmly insist that you be given corrective exercises to take home with you regarding any constraint or limitation they find. Schedule a subsequent assessment every 3-6 months or so to stay on top of changes in your athlete's body.

If you are a parent of a prepubescent pitcher, don't let anyone in the medical community make you feel you are one of those crazed overbearing parents because you want a regular assessment. Of course your athlete's body will change with puberty. That fact goes without saying. However, this young man is pitching in competition NOW—not after some developmental benchmark, and we need to know what his constraints are today.

Imagine your son not getting a report card for his entire 6th grade academic year. Would that be OK with you? I remind you that as a 6th grader he may change his mind any number of times with regards to what he wants to do with his life. Would demanding to see his current grades make you an overbearing parent living your life vicariously through your child? I don't think so! In fact I think it's exactly what a good parent would do. Ditto with getting regular physical assessments.

#2. Strength (Stability) and Mobility/Flexibility. In our pitching athlete, we are looking to create a VERY specific type of strength and mobility/flexibility. Every sport is unique in its requirements. In fact, different positions in a specific sport often have slightly different variations of training theme. Case in point, a quarterback will not train exactly like an offensive lineman, a goalie in soccer will train differently than the midfielder. I'm not suggesting that it is COMPLETELY different. I'm saying that once we have reached our GPP (General Physical Preparedness) our SPP

(Specific Physical Preparedness) is only as good as our understanding of the nuances of that individual's specific skill requirements.

This is where most baseball training falls way short in my opinion. We don't keep asking the next question. We simply throw our pitchers in the weight room with everybody else and do what we've been doing for years and call it "good". It isn't good.

A pitcher's strength balance, symmetry and structural alignment are absolutely critical. Because he will be required to decelerate much more efficiently than any other baseball player on the diamond, he must be consumed with creating strength balance, symmetry, alignment and developing his posterior chain. In essence, developing the parts of a pitcher's body which slow down his arm is actually MORE important than developing the parts of the body which speed up the body.

Dr. Mike Marshall uses a phrase that I totally agree with: "The body will only accelerate itself as efficiently as it can decelerate itself." Therefore I recommend that you follow our lead at The Ranch and work deceleration 3 times as much as you work acceleration.

The conventional wisdom in baseball is that a pitcher needs "balance" to be successful. Of course the traditional teacher of balance is focused on the movement pattern itself and in "finding a balance point". While I personally believe teaching the balance point is absolutely, positively the wrong way to go about things, they are in fact right about how important balance is. They just have incorrectly identified which "balance" is important.

The pitching athlete needs symmetry and alignment. The pitching athlete needs strength balance between accelerators and decelerators.

The pitching athlete needs a balance in specific joints between stability and mobility. If a specific joint lacks mobility, his movements will be limited. If the joint is hyper-mobile, he will lack control of his movements around that joint. The Functional Movement Screen or any assessment by a competent, sports savvy physical therapist will identify these possible issues.

Michael Boyle and Gray Cook approach athletes via what they refer to as the joint-by-joint approach. Long story made short is that while every joint needs a modicum of stability AND mobility, each joint has specific requirements to assist fully in world class performance.

Here is what Boyle and Cook suggest:

The ankle joint needs to be more mobile.
The knee more stable.
The hips more mobile.
The lumbar spine more stable.
The thoracic spine more mobile.
The scapula more stable.
The gleno-humeral (shoulder) more mobile.
The elbow more stable.
The wrist more mobile.

At The Ranch we train with these concepts in the very front of our mind. These sorts of "balances" are absolutely critical to performance. If a pitching athlete is too restricted in his ankle mobility or not stable enough in his knee, it will be very difficult to create a delivery that can perform and repeat at the higher levels of competition over time. Yes, it's THAT important.

Therefore adding strength on top of dysfunction or limitation is a very bad idea. Adding strength in the wrong area is a very bad idea. Likewise, adding range of motion to something already hyper-mobile is a very bad idea.

Two examples of "strong" but wrong for baseball pitchers.

As a baseball pitching athlete, I definitely need mobility and flexibility but I do not need the flexibility of an elite ballet dancer or an Olympic gymnast.

Bottom line: Should my son lift weights or not lift weights? Should he use free weights or machines or just body weight? When should he begin lifting? He also plays football, is his off-season football workout OK or does it hurt him? Should he use the bar or dumb bells or kettle bells? Should he stretch? Should he do Yoga?

Unfortunately I cannot answer any of those general questions for your son. You should stay clear of any outside person who, without assessing your son, offers definitive answers to any of those questions. The truth is that the answer "just depends on the athlete".

What I can tell you is that over 75% of High School players that I have witnessed are not ready for squats in the weight room. Over 50% of all athletes that I observe can't do 10 consecutive perfect pushups. Most do not have the necessary levels of flexibility, mobility and/or stability to perform a forward lunge with a 15 pound ball held over their head. Yet we funnel all these athletes into the same weight room, give them the exact same workout and attempt to build strength. We have all of our athletes circle up and do a group static stretch. Such a process will fail a high percentage of the time because every athlete is not only unique in their present capabilities, they are unique in their constraints and limitations.

Although, Boyle, Gambetta, Cook, Cressey, Weingroff, Fiocchi and I will vary to some degree with regards to the conditioning of pitchers, ALL of us have rejected the standard operating procedure as a flawed process. I suggest you reject it as well and I also suggest you seek out your own expert.

#3. Conditioning/Fitness.

It is here where baseball is actually decades behind other sports.

Here is the traditional baseball pitching conditioning narrative:

- Baseball pitchers need strong legs for power.
- Baseball pitchers need stamina and endurance to pitch for 7-9 innings each start over the 4-5-6 or 7 month season.
- Baseball pitchers need mental toughness because, as we all know, fatigue makes cowards of us all.
- Baseball pitchers need to get the lactic acid out of their system after they pitch.
- Baseball pitchers need to be very fit so their recovery between starts can be accelerated.

The Perfect Answer: Running Poles or Long Distance.

But what if the narrative itself is significantly flawed? What if the very paradigms we based our assumptions on are incorrect? As Einstein was fond of saying, "The way we view the problem may very well be the problem!"

Here is the truth regarding the conditioning of pitchers:

- We all are born with a certain percentage of fast twitch muscle fiber, a certain percentage of slow twitch fiber and a certain percentage of hybrid fiber types which can be converted into either direction. To perform any explosive activity, such as throwing a baseball 95 mph, requires utilization of fast twitch fiber. If we train by utilizing long, medium to slow patterns of movement we encourage the body to recruit the hybrid type of fiber toward the slow twitch. In essence and for the record, while my conclusion is oversimplified for brevity's sake, generally when you train slow...you develop slowness. (Remember the Bernstein Principle?)

79

- All anyone would have to do is compare the physique of the elite sprinter with the physique of the elite long distance runner to see the effects of specific training on muscle fiber recruitment. I ask baseball coaches at every level when they doubt the veracity of my beliefs, to ask  themselves the following question, "You tell me, which athlete you would rather have your pitchers look like?" Enough said.

Still don't believe me? Can you pick out which swimmer is the elite 50 meter freestyle sprinter and which one is the elite 1500 meter long distance swimmer? Obviously the Bernstein Principle applies to swimmers as well: "The body will organize itself based upon the ultimate goal of the activity." If the body's goal is to go fast, it will organize itself to go fast. If the body's goal is to go for a long time, it will organize itself completely differently.

It really is this simple. If you want to train for slow and steady over a long period of time, train like a Pack Mule. They are world class at long and steady over great distances. If you want explosiveness lasting less than 12 seconds, train like a Cheetah.

They are world class in that regard. Unfortunately it is common…even considered exceptional training to train our pitchers like they are Pack Mules and expect them to perform like Cheetahs.

- The physical act of pitching a baseball is accomplished in less than 2 seconds. The athlete then has roughly 20 seconds to recover before he repeats the explosion. Therefore the act of pitching is accomplished entirely inside of the ATP/CP energy system. Training your pitchers by running poles or long distance will do absolutely nothing for their skill specific stamina (the amount of time that a given muscle or group of muscles can perform at maximum capacity).

- So what about recovery? Shouldn't a pitcher take a long run after he pitches to flush out lactic acid and help the body recover faster? Short answer: No. Activities taking less than 2 seconds in duration DO NOT create lactic acid. In fact the long distance run would be the activity that creates the lactic acid. The stiffness the pitcher feels the next day is from the trauma to soft tissue from pitching and the body trying to heal itself. Recovery is very important. A pitcher's recovery can indeed be improved and it is a very important portion of our daily routine at The Ranch. The athlete's level of fitness is definitely a factor in recovery but there are multiple ways to improve fitness and not interfere with the very specific functions a pitcher needs for high level performance.

- And FINALLY, as if all these were not enough to put a wooden stake through the heart of running poles for pitchers, let me give you a few more. Eric Cressey, who not only is a good friend but a great trainer, wrote a series of articles online tackling this specific topic. You can read all of them at: http://www.ericcressey.com/a-new-model-for-training-between-starts-part-1. Let me point out two highlights of Eric's excellent work:

  Long distance running reduces mobility. Simply picture the stride length and arm swing of a marathoner vs. a sprinter. Mobility is vitally important to the pitcher. From a mobility standpoint, running long distance is a poor investment of time and effort.

  Long Distance running has negative effects on our stretch-shortening cycle. In other words it makes us less springy and elastic. Utilizing stored elastic energy is also vitally important for high level performance.

  So in closing this chapter let's return to the conventional view of training and get some clarity.

Here is the tradition baseball pitching conditioning narrative:

- Baseball pitchers need strong legs for power. **That is true, but we will not get the skill specific strength we need as a pitcher by running long distance. The entire concept of skill specific strength as it relates to**

the baseball pitcher needs to be re-evaluated and redefined.

- Baseball pitchers need stamina and endurance to pitch for 7-9 innings each start over the 4-5-6 or 7 month season. **That is true but we will not get the skill specific stamina we need as a pitcher by running long distance. The entire concept of developing stamina as it relates to the baseball pitcher needs to be re-evaluated and redefined.**

- Baseball pitchers need mental toughness because, as we all know, fatigue makes cowards of us all. **That is true, but we will need to develop mental toughness by other means rather than by running long distance.**

- Baseball pitchers need to get the lactic acid out of their system after they pitch. **That is simply not true. The entire concept of recovery as it relates to the baseball pitcher needs to be re-evaluated and redefined.**

- Baseball pitchers need to be very fit so their recovery between starts can be accelerated. **That is true, but we will not get the recovery we need as a pitcher by running long distance.**

Summary Notes of this Chapter for the Parent:

✓ With some degree of earnest work, any average parent can become very familiar with incredible training protocols. There is no shortage of very intelligent people who will give you great direction on skill specific strength and conditioning. Start by studying Michael Boyle, Gray Cook, Eric Cressey, Lee Fiocchi, Vern Gambetta and Dr. Charlie Weingroff.

✓ There is an important distinction between GPP (General Physical Preparedness) and SPP (Specific Physical Preparedness).

✓ For maximum training benefit, the appropriate training must be matched to the appropriate athlete and be based on the athlete's level of readiness and specific point in the competitive season.

✓ Training below an athlete's level of preparedness is mostly a waste of time.

✓ Training above an athlete's level of preparedness places him/her at an increased risk of injury.

✓ Most of baseball, including professional baseball, haven't kept up with or applied much of the latest advancements in training.

✓ Prior to beginning a conditioning program, have a physical assessment completed by a high caliber Physical Therapist, one who works with elite athletes and preferably baseball players.

✓ It's critical to determine any possible constraints, limitations or restrictions in flexibility/mobility, structural alignment, balance, strength and stability.

✓ Request corrective exercises and schedule subsequent assessment every 3-6 months.

✓ Once GPP is reached, one's focus must turn to SPP. This is where most baseball training falls short.

✓ A pitcher's strength balance, symmetry and structural alignment are critical. Developing the parts of a pitcher's body which slow down the arm is MORE important than developing the parts which speed up the body. Mike Marshall: "The body will only accelerate itself as efficiently as it can decelerate itself."

✓ Work deceleration 3 times as much as acceleration.

✓ Pitchers need a balance in specific joints between stability and mobility. Suggestions from Mike Boyle and Gray Cook:

- Ankle joint more mobile
- Knee joint more stable
- Hips more mobile
- Lumbar spine more stable
- Thoracic spine more mobile
- Scapula more stable
- Gleno-humeral (shoulder) more mobile
- Elbow more stable
- Wrist more mobile

✓ Adding strength on top of dysfunction or limitations is a bad idea.

✓ Adding strength in the wrong area is a bad idea.

✓ Adding range of motion to something already hyper-mobile is a bad idea.

✓ Stay clear of any outside person who, without assessing your athlete, offers definitive answers to strength questions.

✓ Baseball is decades behind other sports in pitchers' conditioning and fitness training.

✓ Everyone is born with a certain percentage of fast twitch muscle fibers, a certain percentage of slow twitch muscle fibers and a certain percentage of hybrid muscle fiber types. These hybrids can be converted in either direction. The hybrid types are the critical component. Our goal is to train in a manner that encourages the body to recruit the hybrid toward fast twitch.

✓ If you want slow and steady over a long period of time, train like a Pack Mule.

✓ If you want explosiveness lasting less than 12 seconds, then train like a Cheetah.

✓ Many in baseball train pitchers like Pack Mules and expect them to perform like Cheetahs.

✓ The physical act of pitching a baseball is accomplished in less than 2 seconds with roughly 20 seconds to recover before repeating the explosion.

✓ Activities taking less than 2 seconds in duration DO NOT create lactic acid.

✓ Long distance running is not a good conditioning option for pitchers. It reduces mobility and has a negative impact on the stretch-shortening cycle, making us less springy and elastic. Both mobility and the utilization of stored elastic energy are vitally important for high level performance.

Part II.

There is a Learning Curve

to Everything!

I'm afraid my athlete will never get noticed!

*Straight Talk From
America's "Go-To-Guy"
On Pitching*

Chapter 11

The Truth about a Vast Majority of Lesson Providers

A vast majority of lesson providers are wonderful, caring people. I personally have never met an instructor who wished to harm an athlete or take him/her backward in their skill development. They all have the very best of intentions.

But like almost every other provider of skills or service, only the top 3% of instructors are truly exceptional and world class. The top 10% are very good. The top 25% are solid. The middle 60% tend to be second rate, sloppy, casual and haphazard. The bottom 15% are inept, incompetent and bungling. But you already knew that.

Therefore if you choose an instructor casually or based primarily on location, price or convenience, it would be a stroke of extreme good fortune to land an instructor even in the top 10%. The top 3% almost never can be found without great effort. The law of supply and demand rules supreme here. _why_

Most instructors will market themselves as knowledgeable, competent, high caliber teachers. Therefore you will have to do some research to discover if this person really is the caliber you are seeking. If you needed some critically important, life or death medical or law expertise/advice/direction for your son or daughter, I seriously doubt if you'd look for that person based upon location, price or convenience. Instead, most of you would travel any distance and turn over any stone necessary to find that right advisor. Bottom line: If pitching a baseball is VERY important to your athlete, your choice of teacher/mentor is probably the most critical decision you will ever make. Time is always of extreme value and exceptional teachers are skill accelerators. Buy a cheaper glove if you must, but don't scrimp on your athlete's education. The cost is almost always much too dear.

Chapter 12

The Truth about Select / Travel Ball

Travel ball/select ball is indeed a double edge sword. They are a blessing and a curse. They represent a higher standard of competition and dedication. They represent more commitment in terms of time and money. They elicit higher levels of envy and jealousy. Gone is the feel of neighborhood baseball played with close friends and neighbors. Here to stay is regional.., even in some cases, national recruiting and performance based evaluations. Simply put, baseball now has become a business even for coaches, players and parents of the 10-year-old select/travel ball player.

Gone is playing the game simply for the pure joy of it. Here now is the chasing of national ranking points, showcase events and national championships.

What that means for your pitcher is simply that playing the game of baseball is far more complicated now than it was when you the parent played. It's more complicated physically, but it is also more complicated mentally and emotionally.

My greatest fear with select/travel ball is that young people are damaged mentally/emotionally before they can figure out the game physically. You see, the dirty little secret that very few select/travel ball coaches will admit to is that almost any level of success a player has or fails to have is literally meaningless until the athlete is at a minimum of 15 years of age trying out for his High School team; and in fact, most of the time it is meaningless until they are around 18 years of age.

Until all the athletes have gone through puberty and begin to take the form of the adult they will eventually become, no expert can predict with any certainty who will be the stars at 19 and 21 years of age.

Don't agree with me? Consider these facts. Michael Jordan did not make the varsity basketball cut as a sophomore in High School. Roger Clemens was the 3rd best pitcher heading into his senior season at Spring Woods High School in Houston and had only one scholarship offer, that being to an area Junior college at the conclusion of his senior year. Yet, as we now know, these were not just two decent athletes. These two athletes were two of the greatest athletes of my generation. Yet when they were 16 years old, the world had absolutely no idea how incredible they would become. Therefore, I maintain that if we were not aware of how special these icons were at 16 years of age, what does that say for all the rest of us mere mortals at the age of 16?

Yes, I am well aware of the claims by some in select/travel ball circles that getting "exposure" at 16, 15, 14 and even as young as 13 years old is vitally important to college scholarships or positioning for the professional draft. Whenever I hear such rhetoric, I'm immediately suspicious of how the person forwarding this perception may possibly be profiting financially by marketing this idea to overzealous parents because the evidence is so overwhelmingly to the contrary.

Bottom line: The dedication, discipline and intensity select/travel ball requires can be a very good thing as long as you keep performance in its proper perspective. In your heart of hearts you KNOW in 10 years no one will care if your son won a tournament or a world series. Skill development must be the primary objective and you must never let the side show distract you from that objective.

Use the following as your compass:

- Choose playing time over the most prestigious team.

- Choose development and practice over games and showcases.

- Choose mental/emotional stability and support over drama, "win at all costs" and "what have you done for me lately" organizations.

- Choose mental/emotional stability over revolving door rosters and heavy handed recruiting.

- Choose integrity and class over flashy and loud.

Because at the end of the day, it will be what your athlete is like at 18 and NOT at 8-10-12-14- even at age 16 that will determine how much longer he gets to play the game you're training him for.

Always keep in the front of your mind that select/travel ball is the mode, not the destination. Let it work for you and do not let it become your master.

Chapter 13

The Truth about Year Round Baseball

There is "practice" and then there is "performance". They are definitely NOT one and the same.

Development is about large amounts of deliberate, purposeful, high intensity **practice**. Development is about balance physically, mentally and emotionally. Performance is about the execution of your skill set in a very specific setting. Burn out is created from stagnation and meaningless repetition.

Let me offer you a non-sports scenario as a teaching point. We have a child who is 14 years of age and an aspiring musician. Would it be better in your opinion for the long term development of our young musician to practice every day and perform at an occasional recital or concert or would it be better to spend most of his/her time playing in concerts/recitals and spend far less time practicing?

The answer is obvious. Yet I believe more and more parents are being persuaded by those who profit from their participation to choose performance over practice.

I would admit it is certainly possible to play baseball year round and develop both physically and mentally. It is possible to keep your training balanced and fresh and avoid burn out. But I will tell you I've personally never witnessed any athlete younger than 16 years of age successfully pulling off playing games year round. Personally I've loved baseball my entire life. Today, baseball is my job 24/7 and I'm over 50 years old so I've never gotten burned out on baseball; but I will tell you this—human beings crave variety and freshness. More importantly, they also long for meaning and purpose. I strongly believe that to be successful over the long haul, each athlete must find his own way to create variety, freshness, meaning and purpose.

One of the most common missteps made by otherwise great parents is that they mistakenly believe the key to their athlete's development is "making it possible for their athlete to play in as many games as possible over a 4 or 5 year period." In truth, playing in games rarely makes someone exceptional; only training can do that. I recommend you view games as simply a quiz/test as to how your training is proceeding. School wouldn't be very productive if you took the same or a very similar test every day. Even video games have graduation to different levels fairly close at hand. The same goes for skill development.

Bottom line: Encourage your athlete to play as many sports as he can when he is younger than High School age. He probably will have to begin to narrow his choices in High School. My heartfelt advice is to simply avoid playing organized baseball games 12 months of the year. That doesn't mean you can't play catch or work on your baseball skills all 12 months. I highly encourage that, but I would strongly urge you against playing in games all year long. In my opinion, people get training and performing confused quite often. At the end of the day, it is your quality and quantity of practice that will determine the level of performance.

Chapter 14

The Truth about Showcases, Showcase Camps and Showcase Tournaments

I'm just going to be blunt here. Showcases make sense for only about 15-25% of all baseball athletes actually attending the showcases.

The top 5-15% of all players do not need a showcase. These athletes are going to be noticed and get attention regardless of where they live. Therefore showcases are actually a waste of money for the very top performers. Showcases covet these top athletes because they bring in scouts and other interested parties which in turn bring in the masses who make up a vast majority of the revenue stream.

The bottom 55-65% of all baseball players currently do not have the skills necessary to compete at that next competitive level. Let me be clear. That doesn't mean they NEVER will have those capabilities. It simply means that at this moment in time, they do not. Granted, it is true that a vast majority of them will never develop those abilities; but that is distinctly different in my opinion than the fact that they **currently** do not possess those capabilities.

For example, if you are senior 18 years of age looking to go play in college and you happen to throw the baseball 78 mph (especially if you are a pitcher who is not a knuckleball pitcher), have 78 mph ball exit speed off a tee (as a hitter), have a 2.5+ POP time (as a catcher) and run a 7.5 60 yard dash, I highly recommend you skip the showcase. It will not matter how scrappy you are, how great your attitude or how incredible your baseball acumen. You will be wasting your time and money.

I find so many parents naively believe that the primary reason their son hasn't garnered more attention from college or professional scouts is one primarily of exposure. While that is possible, it is almost never the case. The primary reason is that the athlete lacks the specific skill set required at the next level.

Unless your junior or senior (17-18-year-old athlete) has a minimum 85 mph throwing velocity (especially if he is a pitcher), a minimum of 85 mph ball exit speed, has a POP time under 2.2 (catcher) and/or runs under a 7.0, 60 yard dash, I would not recommend attending a showcase. Exposure is not your athlete's primary problem. Your athlete's problem is a lack of ability/skill. Spend your time, effort and money developing those instead of attending a showcase.

If your athlete is 90+ throwing velocity, 90+ mph ball exit speed, a POP time of 1.9 seconds or less and runs under a 6.7, unless you are from a very rural area, you think your athlete is significantly underexposed or he simply hasn't garnered the interest in a specific school he really wants to attend (and they will be in attendance at the event), I would not recommend attending a showcase. It simply isn't necessary.

I would recommend attending the showcase if you are a junior or senior in HS with a throwing velocity of 85-90 mph or a 85-90 mph ball exit velocity or have a POP time of 1.9-2.2 or run a 60 in 6.8-7.0 and you haven't either garnered a great deal of interest or haven't yet received the specific interest you are wanting. A Showcase in this instance could be very valuable.

Here is the crux of the problem. Most people have very little idea where their athlete stands with regards to these and other measurements. That is a problem because if you don't know, you really have little idea if you should be attending Showcases or if you should instead be focused on developing your skills and abilities. The uninformed parent will therefore be a much easier sell for people who make a profit touting exposure as the answer to all of your athlete's frustrations. As I alluded to previously, those who truly need exposure are about 15-25% of the baseball universe. Showcases can be a very valuable service for those select groups of athletes.

Let me at this juncture offer an additional perspective.

I believe Showcases are potentially valuable in 3 basic ways. I've already discussed the concept of exposure, but I believe there are two ancillary benefits of the Showcase.

I believe Showcases can also be valuable as a test to see where your athlete currently stands with regards to his peer group. In essence, you will find out if your athlete is ahead of the curve, smack dab in the middle or if he is behind.

Showcases can also be good experience to be placed under pressure to perform in front of very large groups of people who are watching, assessing and critiquing.

Many times we live, train and perform in a relatively insulated environment and we may actually fool ourselves into believing that we are better or farther along than we really are. There is often nothing better than an occasional assessment in front of experts and contemporaries with

similar goals and aspirations to jolt us back to reality
us where we really stand and expose our weakne.   ⊔ɪ
flaws.

On the negative side of Showcases, other than it simply being a
poor investment of time and money in your athlete's specific
situation, I commonly see three primary scenarios take shape.
The first one is a situation in which very few people ever see
the negative effects until it is too late.

1) **You are a top prospect and you keep attending Showcases.**
It is a fact of life that familiarity breeds contempt. Often times
the scouts are really enthralled by a player on their first
exposure, but as they see him more and more they begin to seek
and almost always find flaws in his otherwise impressive
veneer. My advice to top prospects is after you become the
"flavor of the month", you become "rare". Rarely does a top
prospect go from a 95 to a 98 on the prospect scale, instead they
inevitably drop.

2) **You are not a top prospect and you do not have a
particularly good showing with the very audience you
are hoping to impress and subsequently, they write you
off as a non-prospect.** It is obviously more difficult to
overcome the resistance of someone who is already
convinced you do not have what it takes than it is to
convince someone who is neutral. My advice is that before
you go to any showcase, have a very good idea what you
need to do to garner interest and be fairly certain you have a
good shot to indeed execute at that level.

3) **You are not a top prospect and you are told in so many words
by the "expert" at the showcase that you simply don't have
what it takes, that you never will and you need to choose**

another path. Because, after all, this guy IS an expert, everyone in this athlete's inner circle, often including himself, could be poisoned into the belief that indeed there is no hope and all is lost. This can really break a person's heart and his spirit which is far more damaging than the simple truth that he is currently behind the specific peer group. Unfortunately this happens every single day not just in baseball but in medicine/health, in education and other forms of activities that require assessment.

Bottom line: Some view me as very anti-Showcase. I am not. **I simply believe you must be very clear on the specific goal(s) of attending the showcase in the first place.** If your goal is exposure, I'd counsel you to do some assessment of your athlete's skill before you attend. I promise you, a majority of athletes who attend Showcases will get little actionable exposure based upon the Showcase.

On a personal note: Our son has been involved for 3 years with the USA Olympic Jr. National Team selection process at his age level. His mother and my goals: 1) To see where our son currently stands with regards to his peer group so we have some clarity as to how to address his future training. 2) To place our son in an environment where he is under pressure to perform in front of very large groups of people who are watching, assessing and critiquing. The possible exposure or making the team are simply ancillary benefits and they are not goals.

Now when Garrett becomes 17 and 18 years of age, exposure may very well become one of the goals, but for now it is not.

Chapter 15

The Truth about High School Baseball

High School Baseball has a potential charm all to itself. For millions of young men and women there may be nothing more fulfilling than playing for their respective high school teams. This is especially true if the team and the sport is passionately followed by the student body and the community. When it's good, high school baseball can be a very rewarding experience. When it's bad, high school baseball can be a living nightmare in the life of a young adult.

As with most things in life, sometimes a thing which should be fairly simple and straightforward can be co-opted by those with an agenda; and they complicate and even possibly ruin something with otherwise great potential for joy, pride and passion.

For that reason, a solid high school coach with integrity is truly worth his weight in gold.

Many youth parents have told me: "We THOUGHT HIGH SCHOOL coaching would have been better!"

My heartfelt advice to parents of any aspiring young high school athlete:

-Don't expect your coach to be baseball's version of John Wooden. That's unfair and unrealistic. Truth be told, you are probably not perfect baseball parents either. Instead expect your coach to simply have personal integrity. The rest you can work through.

-Expect other parents to try to influence or shape situations or circumstances that positively give an advantage to their son. This will almost always be the case. Many otherwise exceptional people will do this unconsciously. Few can deal with their son or daughter with any real objectivity. Sit in judgment of yourself for a moment here. Don't be one of those parents.

-Expect cliques or alliances to be formed in order to increase other individuals' ability to shape or influence. Resist becoming involved in such cliques or alliances to assist your son lest the message be sent to him that the way to get on in life is by manipulating situations to your benefit and/or that you as the parent don't think he has what it takes to overcome obstacles or adversity on his own merits and abilities. This sends the message that you believe he needs YOU to step in. I see this scenario play out quite often, and it is very disempowering to young aspiring athletes. Don't cripple your young athlete by trying to save him from every adversity. Instead support and empower him to work through difficulties. Intervene only when you believe the situation is becoming unhealthy for him physically or mentally/emotionally. Only you can make that decision.

-When the influence works FOR our son, we refer to it as "knowing somebody" or "clout". When it works against our son's interest we call it "politics" and "dirty pool".

-Every coach has a particular strength or a particularly unique skill set as well as a subsequent weakness. Some are good teachers. Some are good motivators. Some are good in a game, others better at practice. Some are too tough, demanding and caustic. Others are too soft, casual and nonchalant. Others don't communicate well. What I highly recommend that you do instead of berating the coach for what he is lacking, is find ways you can supplement his limitations. If your son needs better training, for example, simply obtain it. Do not sit there and stew and complain about what your coach is NOT. Be proactive. The ONLY standard I insist upon for any coach is that he is a man of personal integrity. The other things I can supplement as a parent. Integrity I cannot. The perfect coach does not exist.

High school baseball is seen by some as THE determining factor with regards to college or professional baseball. That may have been the case 20 years ago, but not today. Two of my students in the past 8 years have pitched less than 10 innings with their respective High School teams, yet both received college scholarships to D1 schools. They received their exposure pitching in the summer. While that situation is rare, failing to be a predominate pitcher on your high school staff does not necessarily preclude you from college or professional interest.

On the other end of the continuum I have had 2 pitchers over the past 10 years that have had truly exceptional senior seasons and failed to secure any college or professional interest whatsoever. The reason for this: Simply refer back to my discussion of showcases. While their records and ERA were outstanding, they did not throw the baseball with the necessary velocity to garner interest from the higher levels.

I suggest you view high school baseball as a great opportunity for growth, development and learning that life is far from fair or perfect. It is a fabulous opportunity for young men to learn how to work as a team toward a shared goal without relinquishing personal integrity and independent thought.

Chapter 16

The Truth about Scholarships

It bothers me greatly when I hear a parent tell me their primary interest in their son pitching is to obtain a collegiate scholarship.

In my opinion, you play baseball because you love it. If a university, college or junior college offers to take care of some of your expenses to play for their team, that is a bonus.

In my opinion, you choose a university, college or junior college because you are interested in excelling at a specific academic interest and obtaining a degree from that institution. If this institution happens to have a baseball program that wants you to take part in it while you attend classes; and by being part of that program you can defer some or all the costs, that is a blessing.

If you are fortunate enough that you can marry the two, then that is indeed a tremendous blessing.

Unlike football or basketball, full rides in college baseball are few and far between. Therefore, attending almost any Major D1 institution, especially as an out of state student, you are almost certainly looking at a substantial financial investment even if you are on a 50% scholarship.

The scenarios I see take place so often are of families making decisions based primarily upon the amount of scholarship money or the perceived prestige of the baseball program. It would be far better to choose a place for the athlete to play where he is comfortable with his teammates and coaches and advances in the academic area in which he is sincerely interested. In other words, choose a place where he can best develop as a total human being.

Stanford and Rice University are phenomenal institutions and yet they are certainly far from perfect for everyone. Cliff Lee pitched for Meridian Community College in Mississippi and Justin Verlander for Old Dominion University. Albert Pujols played at Maple Woods Community College. My point is this, if you are good, no matter where you are studying someone will almost certainly find you.

My advice is to choose a place where you can best grow and develop not only as a baseball player but as a student and as a young man. The amount of a scholarship will not matter much in 10 years, but your choices that you make along the way will matter.

As far as obtaining scholarships: Refer back to the showcase segment. It's all about the numbers. Focus on improving your numbers, then the scholarship offers will begin to come your way.

Chapter 17

The Truth about College Baseball

College sports have certainly changed over the past 20 years as well. College athletics is now big business. It used to be that your very best teachers and developers could be found in the collegiate ranks. Today the restrictions placed on the time involved in developing athletes at practice by the NCAA is so strict and severe that true, long-term development really no longer happens at the college level. Recruiting has now become the primary name of the game.

As one might imagine, development takes time. In an effort to allow college student athletes to have more time available to be devoted to the classroom and academic pursuits, the NCAA began placing practice limitations on coaches in the early 1990's.

True development occurs in the off season. The NCAA has steadily gotten more restrictive since 1990 not only in hours per week but also in shortening the time available to be spent in off season.

The result is that most D1 coaches need players to be able to compete and contribute immediately upon arriving at school. They do not have the time for player development. This fact of life definitely skews college recruitment. Coaches are forced into choosing the athlete who will contribute first rather than the athlete who might be considerably better two years from now.

As I alluded to in the previous section, my strong recommendation to parents of an elite baseball player is to choose the college situation in which he feels the most comfortable.

-First, have a genuine affinity for your coaches and teammates. They will be your family for 2-4 years. If you are lukewarm to them coming in, the chances are great that you will be miserable before the season is over.

-Second, be able to play sooner than later. You don't develop much sitting on the bench.

-Third, have a genuine feeling that your coaches like you, believe in you and are excited to have you. Baseball is a game of failure. If your coaches chose you simply to "round out the team" and not as an absolutely necessary cog in the machinery, chances are great that at the first signs of failure you will get the hook and be placed on the shelf. If, on the other hand, you are perceived from the beginning as a vital part of the team and its future, you will get more opportunities to figure things out before the coaches decide your fate.

Chapter 18

The Truth about Being Drafted

The dirty little secret is that if every player who was told they were going to be drafted actually was drafted; the MLB draft would be 5 days instead of 3 days long. Area scouts like to forward the notion that several prospects in their area are leading candidates for the draft. Sometimes they indeed are correct. But far more likely, a vast majority of "prospects" in any one area will never be drafted. So don't fall for the hype and hyperbole. Until the director of scouting for an MLB organization darkens your door, you are probably not going to be drafted.

The draft is simply far more vast than most people realize. You have the entire High School universe, the Junior College universe, the NAIA universe, the NCAA Division III and II universes and the DI Universe. The draft is only 1,240 + picks for that entire set of possibilities.

I have attended MLB Spring Training in both Arizona and Florida for the past 7 straight years and can tell you the number of pitchers throwing in the 87-91 mph range is long and deep in every organization; so it is therefore exceptionally difficult to separate yourself if you are throwing in that velocity range.

If you read pre-draft magazines it is very common to see pitchers being recorded as throwing mid 90's. So why are the mid-90 pitchers all over the magazine but fairly rare at Spring Training? Are they not the same kids?

The short answer is yes, they are the same; and no the scout wasn't exaggerating.

What happens is that when a young starting pitcher enters pro baseball he will pitch every 5 days instead of every 7. His season will expand in length. The strike zone he will pitch to will shrink and the amount of hitters in the line-up he can breeze through shrinks dramatically as well. A base on balls in his past wasn't nearly as costly as it is now. Fewer and fewer hitters are overwhelmed by his fastball or fooled by his off speed offerings.

Through all this, the young professional player begins to understand how critical location and pitch sequencing is and his focus on velocity typically begins to wane. To complicate matters, many professional organizations de-emphasize long toss and other activities that they believe can place extra stress on the arm/shoulder/elbow. And as the Bernstein Principle would suggest, the body begins to organize itself differently.

Professional baseball has come to accept this drop in the average fastball velocity as simply a normal phenomena. Therefore many organizations actually prefer big, physical pitchers who throw in the mid 90's so that after a pitcher loses his subsequent 2-3 mph in his first two years of pro ball, "theoretically" he can still be throwing in the low 90's.

So what does all that have to do with the draft and your pitching athlete?

If you are right handed and are shorter than 6'2", you are going to have to throw in the mid 90's to generate any interest in the MLB draft. That is regardless of what your area scout will tell you to the contrary. MLB organizations simply don't think your size can withstand the rigors of a professional season and maintain your velocity. This is especially true if you appear to be up tempo and very ballistic (what the pro scouts refer to as "max effort").

Lincun !

If you are left-handed and shorter than 6'2", you are given a small velocity break of 2-3 mph over your right handed peer.

If you are taller than 6'3" and have a large frame, you are also given a small velocity break over your faster moving, more dynamic smaller/shorter peers because the narrative is that the bigger athlete has a potentially higher upside as he learns to use his body.

Is their reasoning sound? I don't believe it is. I see no evidence to support such a paradigm; but as we all know, perception is reality and such a mindset is very prevalent in MLB. You should simply be aware of this thought process going into the draft and into professional baseball.

Chapter 19

The Truth about Professional Baseball

Professional baseball is not the magical spectacle most see on television. Of course neither are most sports and other forms of entertainment when you look behind the curtain. Baseball is a tough, extremely competitive, ruthless business where there is very little room or patience for error and even less loyalty.

It is common knowledge inside MLB circles that players drafted after the 3rd round have relatively little chance of ever making it to the Major Leagues. In fact only a portion of players in the first three rounds ever play in a big league game. Certainly players like Mike Piazza (62nd round), Roy Oswalt (23rd round), and Albert Pujols (13th round) prove that one can be a star regardless of where they are drafted but the odds grow longer as the picks get higher.

Because of that, most draftees are thought of as simply filler to be utilized; because after all, someone has to pitch and hit to the inevitable stars as they climb their way up to take their rightful place on MLB rosters. The "stars" obviously have to play with and against somebody.

Because of this harsh reality, based on the sheer numbers that do not make it, most of MLB subsequently believes in the "freak theory" which basically accepts as fact that the ones who do make it are simply genetically superior to the ones who do not.

I will tell you why, in my opinion, the freak theory is so widely accepted.

Every year at Spring Training the cupboards of each organization are overflowing with athletes trying to break camp with one of 6 teams. The MLB club, AAA, AA, high A, short season A, and Rookie Ball. Dozens of athletes will be released in the course of Spring Training as the music around April 1 stops and only so many chairs are left remaining. That is a painful time for everybody. No one likes to tell a young man that the dream he has held next to his heart since childhood has come to an abrupt end.

To ease that pain, many coaches have convinced themselves that the selection process is simply following fate. Either someone was gifted ENOUGH, or he wasn't. The athlete's release had absolutely nothing to do with their personal inability to teach, reach or shape movement patterns. It simply wasn't meant to be.

The athlete also finds it easier to accept things by buying into the "freak theory" as well. In other words, if Justin Verlander made it and I did not, it was simply because Verlander was especially gifted or endowed by his Creator and I got the short end of the stick. It certainly wasn't because he worked harder or smarter that I did. Verlander was simply a "Freak".

Believing in the "Freak Theory" offers both groups—players and coaches—cover.

The belief system most in MLB operate under can be distilled down to a single phrase. "One either has 'IT' or one doesn't, and if you have to actually work too hard on getting 'IT', it almost certainly means you don't have 'IT'."

So what does that have to do with you? Unless you are drafted very high, understand that the organization actually views you as having very little chance of making it to the Big Leagues and that your spot is untenable and very temporary.

If you are drafted fairly high and the organization invested some significant money into you, you have a much larger window of opportunity but it still is far more finite that many realize.

Bottom line: If you are ever lucky enough to get to pro ball, KNOW that your clock is ticking and you'd best show up ready to demonstrate your very best stuff immediately. Getting to professional baseball isn't the end of the process; it is the beginning of a whole new game and one that they play for keeps.

Part III.

What is so unique about the philosophy

of

Ron Wolforth's

Texas Baseball Ranch

and

**How can I or my athlete gain or benefit from what you
do at The Ranch?**

*Straight Talk From
America's "Go-To-Guy"
On Pitching*

Chapter 20

<u>The Athletic Pitcher™ Pyramid</u>

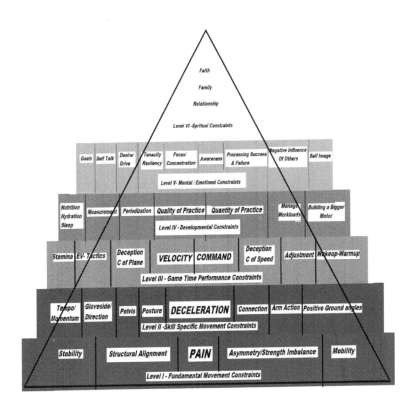

This illustration gives the reader a visual representation of how we view training and development at the Texas Baseball Ranch. The primary Ranch difference is simply that we begin with a completely different paradigm. We are holistic in our approach. Simply look no further than the foundation of the pyramid. Our training foundation is comprised of stability, mobility, asymmetries, alignment, strength balances and we BEGIN with the centerpiece of it all—pain. If our pitching athlete has pain, tightness, tenderness or even fatigue, we go no further until that is addressed. In fact, our attention to pain is one of seven primary differences that separate The Ranch from other schools, training facilities or academies.

The 7 Primary Things That Separate The Ranch

- We START with the pain

- We reject the "One Size fits All" One Ideal Mechanical Model

- We reject the Genetic Freak Theory

- We understand recovery and consistency are absolutely critical elements to long-term success

- We build a bigger motor absolutely specific to pitching

- We are obsessed with getting your BEST stuff in the zone 75% of the time

- We develop a World class Mindset and a Mental Management System

Let me briefly discuss the vital importance of each one.

1. We START with the pain

There may possibly be nothing more profound than this first paradigm and when I say we **start** with the pain, I mean regardless of whether the pitcher is 8 years old or 38 years of age, we begin here, with this assessment.

Ron Wolforth's Texas Baseball Ranch™

Initial Pitching Questionnaire and Phase I Assessment

Name of Athlete_____

Date of Birth_____/_____/_____

Height_____'/_____" Weight_____

Began pitching at age of_____

When I currently have pain, soreness, tenderness, tightness, stiffness or <u>even simple fatigue</u>: it occurs in one of these 5 areas (You must choose 1)

Pain Algorithm

_____Medial elbow

_____Lateral Elbow

_____Anterior (Front) Shoulder

_____Posterior (Back) Shoulder

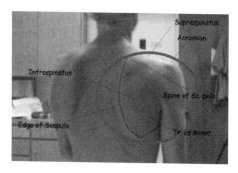

_____Multiple Sites

_____Medial Elbow

_____Lateral Elbow

_____Anterior Elbow

_____Posterior Elbow

Why do we start here? Simple. This assessment gives us insight into the individual's weakest link. Unless and until we solve this issue ALL the rest of our pitching goals and objectives will be by far more difficult / impossible to obtain including:

- Velocity

- Command

- Movement

- Changing speed

- Recovery/ Consistency

Eliminate the pain...and

- The body will allow us to throw harder

- The body will allow us to throw more often

- We will recover more quickly

Before we become a prolific PITCHER...we must first become a prolific THROWER!

Fail to address the pain...and

Our body will 1) morph itself/organize itself to reduce the pain...or 2) we will BREAK...usually in the soft tissue surrounding a joint (shoulder/elbow).

Our goal is to quickly identify the possible contributors to the Pain, or in other words find out what is keeping an athlete from currently having a healthy, durable, electric arm.

Possible Contributors include:

✓ **Type I contributors-Structure Related**

- Physical misalignments, asymmetries, strength imbalances, constraints in mobility/flexibility and/or strength/ stability

✓ **Type II contributors-Movement Pattern Related**

- The movements related to actually throwing the ball

✓ **Type III contributors-Workload / Recovery Related**

- How much, how long, how often, how many per inning, how quickly you return to full speed

✓ **Type IV contributors-Training Related**

- How your training process itself is affecting your abilities

✓ **Type V contributors- Internal Systemic Related**

- Sleep, Nutrition, Hydration

When we identify the possible contributors to that pain and systematically address those, the results are often nothing short of spectacular. Much like when a ballast is reduced on a hot air balloon, the athlete quite often takes off and never looks back.

You see, often it's not that you need to do something completely different, it's identifying and addressing what is currently constraining you that is critical. Most parents and athletes simply never have that conversation or sit down and make that evaluation. They keep doing the same thing over and over again and this time, expecting a different result.

2. We reject the "One Size fits All" One Ideal Mechanical Model

Almost every week I get a request from someone who would like for me just to give them a *"schedule"*. Do this on Monday. Do this on Tuesday. Hold the ball like this. Lift your leg like this. THEN, you'll be as good as rain.

It's not really their fault. They have simply accepted the premise that there is one perfect way to do something, and they think I just might be the guy who has figured this whole thing out.

I actually get a chuckle out of one fairly prominent internet pitching guru who claims to have cold hard science behind his methodology. REALLY?

You mean we are still debating the origin of the universe, global warming, the efficacy of evolution, is coffee and oat bran actually good for us or not; but as far as pitching a baseball...well THERE he has it ALL figured out. Please. Give me a break.

If you want to work with someone who apparently has this all figured out, by all means put down this book and look this gentleman up on the internet. He is not hard to find. As for me, I'm fairly certain I don't even have all the questions yet, let alone all the answers.

What I do know is that no two pitchers in MLB history have ever thrown identically. EVER! Therefore I believe we must look at each pitcher as an individual. That doesn't mean there are not universal principles that apply; there are.

As I tell the people who request a schedule that as soon as I write ONE schedule or one process, here is what happens: "Well, that doesn't quite fit… This one thing won't work… This particular item doesn't apply… I don't have that much time…or don't have that piece of equipment."

So, in other words, the instant the ink is dry on the schedule it needs to be revamped or altered to fit the specific needs of the individual. Ten years ago I tried to work through that process. Now I know it is a true waste of my time.

Instead, we find what you need to address individually. Then we attack those constraints within the limitations of your life, like time, space, equipment and resources available. We then look at the results and modify the process accordingly.

One size will not only fail to fit everyone, one size won't even fit ONE forever. Your process will need to change as you change.

I joke with my clients all the time. "Why are the desks in 3rd grade so small?" Answer: "Because you are not supposed to stay there." My obvious message is that the Good Lord designed you to constantly grow, adapt, learn, expand, not for you to strictly follow some arbitrary cookie cutter process.

So why then do so many people adhere to the ideal mechanical model and a very strict choreography?

Simple really, if you take time to think about it. It's easier on THEM. They are not required to think, adjust or adapt. They simply follow.

Thomas Edison once said, "It amazes me the lengths to which the average person will go to avoid conscious thought."

I believe the choice is rather simple. Either A) believe in the one size fits all method and then be in constant search for the program or guru of the month with the perfect recipe and hope he can lead you to the promised land or B) reject one size fits all and really go to work at identifying and addressing the individual limitations, constraints or road blocks that are keeping you personally from your ultimate destination.

3.   We reject the Genetic Freak Theory

I've already discussed the "Freak theory" at length so I will be brief here.

Do we REALLY think successful people have a special genetic makeup and or are freaks of nature? Many people truly believe this.

I don't believe it for one moment. History is filled with examples of ordinary people who were once thought of as colossal failures succeeding far beyond any of their critics' wildest imaginations.

I will give you five examples myself and if after reading these five you still believe in the "freak theory" then I believe you are a hopeless cause.

1.   Michael Jordan. Cut as a sophomore from his varsity HS basketball team.

2. Roger Clemens. The 3rd best pitcher heading into his senior season at Spring Woods HS in Houston, Texas. His only college scholarship offer was to San Jacinto JC.

3. Faith The Dog—the only dog in the world that walks upright like a human.

4. Lu Wei—Chinese piano player with no arms wins "China's Got Talent" competition playing the piano with his feet.

5. Scott Kazmir—In 2002, Scotty was the talk of MLB organizations. During his senior season he threw 4 straight no hitters. He was drafted in the first round by the NY Mets; and at the ripe age of 22 years, 2 months and 10 days, Scott became the youngest opening day starter since Dwight Gooden in 1986. On June 2006, Scott passed Sandy Koufax and put himself in the 22nd spot in MLB for most strikeouts by a lefthander before his 23rd birthday. Scott led the American League in Strikeouts with 239. By 2011 Scott was released from baseball and since 2012 has been working with me trying to return to MLB. His progress over this span has been slow but steady, and I believe he will return fairly soon back to the MLB.

Athletes 1 and 2. Surely two of the greatest athletes of my generation would have shown signs of their incredible genetic superiority before their 15th birthday? The truth is not only were these two not at the top of the heap from a perspective of their national peer group at 15 years of age, they were not the best at THEIR own high School.

Athlete 3. We all know that every dog that has been on planet earth for the past several thousand years has walked on four legs not two. Certainly Faith's genetic blueprint of four legs walking would be more than set in stone. Yet this animal walks on two legs, not BECAUSE of her genetics but IN SPITE of her genetic blue print. So if you don't know the story, you might wonder why Faith walks on two legs. The answer is because she has to. She was born without her two front paws. It is simply amazing what can be done when it HAS to be done. God is great!

By the way, several experts suggested early on that Faith could NEVER learn to walk on two legs. Her skeletal structure was not meant to walk that way. Come to find out the experts were again wrong, Faith did learn to walk and her bone structure modified itself to support her movements. Imagine that. (Bernstein Principle anyone?)

Athlete 4. Lu Wei lost his two arms in an accident at 10 years old. But Lu truly loved music and wanted to learn to play the piano with his feet. Seven different piano instructors told Lu his goal was unattainable because the toes just don't have the dexterity or coordination to play an instrument like the piano. So Lu had to teach himself.

Once again the "experts" were wrong. Lu not only learned to play the piano, he learned to play it so well he won a national talent show. So the question is, "Did Lu Wei have superior genetics?" I believe it to be an absurd question. As I mentioned earlier, it is simply amazing what can be done when it HAS to be done. God is great!

Athlete 5. Many of you might be saying, "OK, Coach we've got you now. Doesn't Scott doing so well so early prove the freak theory?"

Here is my point. Scott's genetic makeup didn't change in the past five years. Other things did—things that are FAR more critical to performance.

In fact I believe it was many of Scott's coaches who accepted the freak theory and the one size fits all theory that hurt Scotty. Instead they should have addressed Scott's individual needs, constraints, limitations and PAIN every step of the way. Had they done that, it is my opinion Scott would still be an All-Star caliber pitcher today.

I believe Scott's de-evolution of sorts is yet another proof positive that success is not about genetics.

4. **We understand recovery and consistency are absolutely critical elements to long-term success**

The most effective way I have been able to have my Minor League clients understand the importance of this topic is to show them two lists.

List A	List B
Dallas Braden	Grover Cleveland Alexander
Anibal Sanchez	Greg Maddux
Bud Smith	Steve Carlton
Eric Milton	Roger Clemens
Jose Jimenez	Tom Glavine
Chris Bosio	Lefty Grove
Joe Cowley	Whitey Ford

I then ask them to tell me the significance of those two lists. Most have no idea. A vast majority of my clients have a difficult time even identifying anyone on list A.

The answer is list A are MLB pitchers who have thrown a no-hitter in the major leagues. List B are pitchers who never threw a no-hitter in the major leagues.

My point? Long-term success rarely is about "stuff". Obviously to get out 27 MLB hitters without one of them getting a hit would indicate that, at least on THAT day, the pitcher had exceptional 'stuff'.

True, long-lasting success is about being good on a regular basis instead of being unhittable once or twice in a career. Therefore a pitcher's ability to pitch a game and recover well enough five days later to be "good" again is critically important.

At The Ranch, developing individual processes for recovery is a priority.

5. We build a bigger motor absolutely specific to pitching

Every High School and college has a weight room and a strength program. Some of them are very, very good. Most are not.

It is far too simplistic to suggest that too many programs have a football paradigm of lifting. In fact some of what football does is exceptional for baseball and we all know that Peyton Manning and Tom Brady don't utilize the exact same program that their offensive linemen and defensive lineman do. Why? Because even in football, each position is skill specific.

The key here is that your workout is specific to the exact skill you are performing AND specific to your personal needs, strengths and limitations.

I classify my athletes into 4 categories:

- Primarily needing mobility/flexibility - strength/stability is not an issue

- Primarily needing strength/stability - mobility/flexibility is not an issue
- Needs BOTH strength/stability AND mobility/flexibility
- Is very Balanced, maintain present course

The critical thing to remember in developing your training regimen is that pitching a baseball is a 2 second explosion followed by 20 seconds of rest, repeated in 5-9 sets of 15-20 explosions with a half inning of recovery (10-15 minutes) in between sets. Therefore we must train explosively and build our recovery into the natural flow the athlete experiences in a game.

6. We are obsessed with getting your BEST stuff in the zone 75% of the time

Simply stated it will not matter if our athlete throws the ball 100 mph or has devastating off speed stuff, if he can't get his pitches consistently in the zone, we are wasting our time and doomed to failure.

Our process is simple. Our standard is 75%. Your goal is to get your CURRENT best stuff in the zone 75% of the time. Why 75%? Because 50% means you are constantly in trouble. 66% means you are really forcing the hitter's hand and if you train at 75% in practice, you are assured to be very good when you are in the heat of battle with all of its chaos and anxiety.

Roy Halladay and Cliff Lee are routinely between 70-75% in the zone. This is what we believe all of our athletes should aspire to, THEN we go to work at improving our current stuff.

7. We develop a World class Mindset and a Mental Management System

Although this difference is listed last out of seven, I believe that after assessing the pain, the athlete's mindset and managing his thoughts and emotions are more important than almost anything else in determining his eventual level of achievement.

At The Ranch, we dedicate 15 minutes of every session exclusively to mindset and then intertwine the mental management into all of our training processes.

I suggest "*With Winning in Mind*" by Lanny Bassham to get you started on the process.

Part IV.

Final Pieces of Advice

Common Sense is unfortunately not common.

Straight Talk From
America's "Go-To-Guy"
On Pitching

Conclusion

Final Pieces of Advice

If you do what everybody else does, you are going to get what everybody else gets.

When I was quite young I vividly remember driving home with my father from his work in the summer; and every afternoon at 5:05 pm, Earl Nightingale would come on KIMB radio and tell his nationally syndicated audience about "The Strangest Secret". The basis of his message was basic common sense.

I remember one message in particular that really resonated with me even at 12 years old. Mr. Nightingale stated that being "mediocre" or "average" simply meant that whatever the topic, most people followed a specific path. If you wanted to be exceptional, he counseled, you must find out what everyone else was doing and choose to do something quite different.

As the great philosopher Forrest Gump used to say, "Stupid is as stupid does!" I would add; "Average/mediocre is what average/mediocre does."

The reason I constantly remind my clients of this "secret" is that by deciding on a different path, they will be belittled, besmirched, criticized, made fun of and ridiculed by what I refer to as the "soft, envious, lazy, confused, indecisive, mediocre middle".

To be honest, if you aren't getting criticized by this group on a fairly regular basis, I would personally begin to question whether or not I was far enough off the "mediocre path".

If you do what you've always done, you are going to get what you've always gotten.

Remember Albert Einstein's definition of insanity?

"Insanity is doing the same thing over and over again and this time expecting a different result."

Einstein's definition should be placed in everybody's home or office to remind us that if we are not currently getting the results we are seeking, we need to adjust our sails. Adjust. Modify. Adapt.

I certainly know 31 MLB teams that desperately need Einstein's words in front of them on a regular basis. Several of them are what I refer to as "stuck on stupid".

I remind all my professional clients in our first meeting together every winter: "Fellas, not only are we not doing what everybody else is doing—so for you new guys that certainly means we won't be doing what you are used to doing—in fact we are not going to be doing what we did last year. We are better this year. We have better information. While last year our information was indeed world class, the way one STAYS world class is to be constantly improving and evolving our process. Gentlemen, the good adjust. The GREAT adjust quickly and seamlessly because that is who they are. We aspire to be GREAT."

As with everything else in life, it all comes down to knowledge and education.

I remind my son and daughter often that almost any problem or obstacle has already been solved or its solution created by someone else and all you need to do is seek out and find that person or group.

The Holy Bible states quite clearly, "Seek and You shall find. Ask and it will be given unto you."

With the internet there truly is no reason that you can't find a solution to almost any significant issue or problem. If you have read this far through the book, I'm fairly certain you already look at things differently than before you started. I hope that difference is one of clarity and a wider perspective. That's at least what I was aiming for in writing this book.

As with everything else in life, it all comes down to finding just the right person/expert/mentor.

Personally I have many mentors. I have two mentors with regards to marketing and business development. I have several mentors when it comes to issues with physical therapy and rehab for pitchers. I have two mentors who are orthopedic surgeons and advise me on injury creation and reduction. I have several mentors with regards to strength and conditioning for my pitchers. I have several mentors with regards to sports psychology and mental conditioning. I rely heavily on two close, personal colleagues with regards to mechanics and movement patterns. The list goes on.

Why would I feel the need for such a large number of mentors in various fields? Because I know one can only be expert in a very finite set of areas. There is a learning curve to every course of discovery and sometimes that learning curve is long and/or steep. If I can find someone who has already climbed that slope then I would be foolish not to utilize and plug into that knowledge, expertise, experience and wisdom.

My strong advice to you is to do the same in every area or aspect that is important to you.

Some people respond to me, "…but Coach isn't that expensive?"

My response: Not nearly as expensive as not doing it and spinning my wheels in the mud until I figure it out, which may NEVER happen. If it's important, I do not miss the chance to get a mentor who either has been where I want to go or has a track record of helping others get to where I want to go.

As with everything else in life, it all comes down to ACTION vs. intentions, feelings or thoughts.

Finally it comes down to taking action. Knowledge isn't enough. Thoughts aren't enough. Great intentions are not enough.

This is where most young athletes ultimately fail. They simply stay on their current path because it is comfortable and HOPE things turn out better. Hope is not a plan.

An athlete is where he is precisely because of the decisions and actions he has made up until this moment in time. The great news is that the present doesn't have to equal the future. Anyone can change their future in an instant. Just DECIDE. Carpe Diem, Good luck and May God Bless your Path.

Coach Wolforth

Epilogue
Who Are You—Exactly?

In my opinion there are several very important questions you should frequently ask yourself:

Who am I?

What do I stand for?

What do I believe in?

And if a situation arises that challenges or tests those sensibilities,

What am I prepared to do about this?

For most people unfortunately, the answer to that question is to complain, whine, moan, play the victim or simply "go along to get along".

My family and I are not unlike a vast majority of you reading this. We don't want or like unnecessary drama in our life. We are far from perfect. We don't seek out confrontation. We don't gain pleasure or energy from ticking other people off or making enemies of our neighbors.

Instead we long for cordial relationships and harmony. We want to be liked, admired and respected. But sometimes the circumstances in front of us force us to choose between who we are and conforming to or accepting the current path placed in front of us by others.

How prepared are we to stand by the power of our convictions—especially when those positions happen to be unpopular and/or come with an obvious cost or consequence?

I share this particular story so that some of you may be able to gain strength or support from my family's experience.

A vast majority of you have heard or used the phrase, "You can't fight city hall!"

The inference is that the bureaucracy is too large for a single person to challenge. If a single entity challenges a corporation or a large bureaucracy, many times that large entity will move to literally steam roll or squash the non-conformist. Non-conformity, resistance or defiance of the path or process of this entity is often considered insubordination, rebellion, sedition and even treachery/treason and reacted to very harshly and occasionally dealt with extreme prejudice. The entity is simply too powerful to be challenged by those they view as pawns or foot soldiers.

This method of rebellion squashing has been used since the beginning of man to keep the masses in line and keep the specific culture from chaos and anarchy.

However, many times the culture at large and specifically the large bureaucracy is headed in the wrong direction and the only thing saving it from tyranny or driving off a cliff are courageous individuals who are willing to step up to the plate and risk the spears and arrows thrown at them by the "bureaucracy".

Our story begins at the United States Specialty Sports Association (USSSA) 11 and under Baseball World Series in Orlando, Florida. My son's team is in the Final 8 and we are playing the first game in the morning of the final two days. I take my regular position in center field away from everyone, sat down in my lawn chair and got comfortable.

In the middle of the first inning our coach made a pitching change. The shortstop was brought in to pitch and received 3 warm-up pitches and the game resumed. I immediately got out of my chair and went to the dugout to inquire exactly why only 3 pitches were allowed. I was informed the home plate umpire simply decided we were going to go to 3 pitches warm-ups at all times for the remainder of the game to make certain we stayed on time.

I immediately left to find the tournament director. Instead I found the assistant tournament director. Her response was that my coach had been told at the beginning of the tournament this could happen and that the number of warm-up pitches would be at the umpire's discretion. When I insisted that this was simply not an acceptable situation from a health perspective, she simply told me "the rule was the rule" and I needed to take it up with my coach not her...and in her opinion I needed to "get over it and move on".

The arrogance and elitism of this individual surprised even me. This was her universe and I was simply in it.

Of course remember...this organization is "ALL about the kids".

I got her name and moved on.

The 3 pitch warm-up rule was enforced for the remainder of the game.

When I returned home I sent an e-mail to several higher ups in the USSSA organization expressing my displeasure and why this decision of theirs actually placed young arms at unnecessary risk. I offered my expertise in establishing standards for warm-up in pitchers.

First, I received an e-mail stating that I had my facts wrong and that the 3 pitch warm-up rule was never instituted and they followed the MLB standard of 8 pitches for a new pitcher in the game or a pitcher's first inning and 5 pitches per inning after that.

I responded with exact names and places and insisted that I indeed had my facts correct.

Several e-mails later I received an e-mail from the legal representative of USSSA and through him the tone had turned nasty quickly. It was clearly a shot across my bow. His general message: Drop this immediately or we will respond to your threats by whatever means at their disposal.

I assured them I was not making threats. I am not a litigious person. I was 50 years old at the time and had never even thought of filing suit against anyone my entire life and this was no exception. Their organization had simply made a mistake and that error would place young men at unnecessary risk and my expertise made me uniquely qualified to assess this situation. Period! End of story.

All I wanted was assurance that this situation would not happen again or I would feel compelled to recommend that my son, his team and anyone I would come in contact with simply not play in USSSA events.

I truly thought the matter was a very simple one. It was an obvious mistake. We ALL make mistakes. I thought USSSA would simply admit to it, adjust and move on. I didn't expect a thank you for bringing this to their attention. After all, I even offered my assistance for heaven's sake.

But most of you already know that saying "oops" is not how big bureaucracies typically behave. The "Big Dogs" don't often say they are wrong. Most of the time their reaction is: "Who do you think YOU are challenging XYZ Corporation or the federal, state or local government? We'll show you who is in charge here you little silly person. You'll rue the day you messed with us."

I told my wife, "Jill, this could get ugly. These people are obviously not interested in getting this right. They are far more concerned with maintaining their perceived power and control and believe we are threatening that power. If we stand pat they almost certainly will ban Garrett and Garrett's team from USSSA events. That is their only POWER play here but I believe we must do this. If we don't stand up to this nonsense what chance would the normal everyday Dad and Mom have in facing them?"

We then warned Garrett's team and coaches that we were not backing down and explained the possible blow back that could occur.

The team and coaches were VERY supportive of our position.

Several days later the USSSA did impose their nuclear option. The Wolforth's received a lifetime ban from participating in USSSA events unless the USSSA received a letter from our legal representative that we would not sue the USSSA.

We have NOT moved one inch in pursuing such a letter and we are completely content that the USSSA ban will remain a lifetime ban. In fact we view our ban proudly as a badge of courage.

The Wolforth family believes we should constantly remind ourselves "Who are our friends?", "Who are our adversaries?", "What do we believe?", and "What do we stand for?" We feel quite comfortable counting USSSA as one of those groups we stand firmly in opposition to in regards to this specific issue. While there definitely was a personal cost to standing by our position, we believe it is a price we will gladly pay any time if we must.

Many people have asked me that if we had to do it all over again would we choose the same path.

That answer is, "Absolutely!" I wouldn't change one thing.

Jill and I truly believe:

"Adversity doesn't develop character so much as it reveals it."

Always keep that in mind as you pursue excellence.

Stay curious and keep fighting the good fight.

Coach Wolforth

Ron Wolforth's
Texas Baseball Ranch Presents
The NEW Athletic Pitcher™ Program

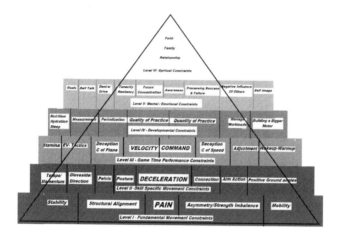

The Biggest Lie in Baseball:

You are either born with 'it' - or you aren't…and if you have to work on 'it'…that means you don't have 'it'.

I've got a confession to make to all you pitchers, coaches and parents out there…I once believed a player had to have "it" in order to become a star pitcher... and I honestly believed you were either born with "it" - or you weren't.

But today the thought that it's "all about your genes" makes me laugh

Over the course of my 27 years coaching and training players, I have witnessed pitchers – *from little league to professional baseball* – make amazing transformations in their game.

And <u>NONE</u> of these transformations had anything to do with their genes.

- I have seen really solid pitchers – *with just a few minor trouble spots* – **completely lose their athleticism and their mental game**. All because they tried to use the old, conventional, "one-size-fits-all" training programs... and it interfered with "what made them special in the first place".

- And I have personally helped some pretty troubled pitchers identify all their trouble spots, eliminate their constraints and **become truly exceptional pitchers** (who landed the attention of big-name scouts and college coaches).

Over the years, I completely changed my mind on "conventional" training and techniques, and now I want to change your mind, too.

Back in 1999 I started realizing that ANY PITCHER can improve their velocity, speed, control, mobility, flexibility and strength.

When I changed my mindset and stopped believing the old, conventional way was the only way... truly amazing things started to happen at my **Baseball Ranch in Montgomery, Texas**.

The Results We Achieved:

- **64** of our athletes have been drafted

- **4 Major League Pitchers**

- **114** pitchers have touched 90 MPH

- **16** have touched 95 MPH

- **2** have touched 100 MPH

Trevor Bauer
The #3 overall draft pick in 2011 draft
(drafted by the Arizona Diamondbacks)

With The *NEW Athletic Pitcher*™ Program You Can Prove To The World You Are More Than A Set of Genetic Blueprints

You too **CAN** become a better pitcher. You can become a stronger, more explosive pitcher. And I can promise you one thing… you can start playing at a level that most of your other coaches and trainers don't believe is possible for you to play at. Believe me; I have seen it happen over and over again.

"The original "Athletic Pitcher™*" program was groundbreaking for velocity enhancement. Ron Wolforth's new program goes way beyond that. The strength of what happens on a daily basis at the Texas Baseball Ranch is the continuing search for the best throwing and conditioning information available from reliable sources. The "New Athletic Pitcher*™*" DVD series is an easy to understand compilation of those sources. I strongly recommend this series if you are serious about your son's health and ongoing development as a thrower and pitcher."*

Brent Strom
Minor League Pitching Coordinator, **St. Louis Cardinals**

The "*New Athletic Pitcher*™" is the most comprehensive program on pitching that I have ever seen. Not only does it show you the most practical, fundamental sound way to address issues in your pitching delivery, it is absolutely the best program for arm health and durability. **On top of all that, The "***New Athletic Pitcher***™" program is truly revolutionary in the way it shows you how to prepare physically for the demands of pitching. I use the program to prepare all my pitchers at Weatherford College, because the bottom line is, IT GETS RESULTS!!!**

Flint Wallace
Pitching Coach, **Weatherford College**

For more information or to purchase the Program:

www.TheAthleticPitcher.com

NOTES

The Exclusive, 3-Day Baseball Pitching Camp for Committed Pitchers Who Have a Burning Desire to Advance to the Next Level

Ron Wolforth's Elite Pitchers Boot Camp:
3 Days of the Most Intense, Results-Driven Pitching Instruction, Training and Education in the Country Today.

My coaches and I all BELIEVE *without a doubt* that every kid can reach 90 mph.

We have seen it happen time and time again *(by kids who were told they would NEVER reach 80mph, much less 90mph)*. All you need to become a great pitcher is the right information, the right training and the right work ethic.

If you – or your son - have the dedication and the desire to become an unstoppable pitcher, then my **Elite Pitcher's Boot Camp** will supply you with the knowledge and the training you need to reach any pitching goal.

147

#3 Draft Pick for 2011 - Trevor Bauer On Elite Pitchers Boot Camp...

"Participating in the weekend '**Elite Pitchers Boot Camp'** was the best decision I have ever made for my baseball career.

The information provided opened the door to a path that has transformed my career and allowed me to achieve my lifelong dream of becoming a professional baseball player."

Trevor Bauer
2011 Golden Spikes Award Winner
#3 Draft Pick 2011 Draft
Arizona Diamondbacks

With over 64 of my students drafted in the past 9 years, I have learned something that changed my life (and the lives of the pitchers I coach). I have learned that in order to get Life-Changing Results, you have to think outside the box and do things a little differently. This is why I designed the **Elite Pitchers Boot Camp** to be a completely different type of Pitching Camp.

Here, the focus is on the individual player.

We will assess your strengths, identify your weaknesses and then you will discover what areas you need to focus on to develop a plan of action that WILL transform you into a stronger, more mental, more powerful pitcher.

I have held over **110 Elite Pitchers Boot Camps** and worked with thousands of pitchers… and the results are truly something to brag about.

WARNING:
The Elite Pitchers Boot Camp is <u>NOT</u> for 90% of the People Reading This Page.

- The Ranch is **far more intense** than anything most pitchers have ever experienced

- The Ranch is <u>not air conditioned for comfort</u> and doesn't have shiny new equipment or state of-the-art machines because we KNOW *it's the right information – not the right equipment –* that will take you to the next level.

- **The Ranch isn't a nanny.** We won't force anything upon the athlete. We give you freedom to develop what works best for you.

- The Ranch <u>doesn't clone, cookie cut, choreograph</u> or give you a one size fits all system for you to follow.

- The Ranch **doesn't talk down to you**, arrogantly assume we know what is best for you or dictate your every move and thought.

The only things at The Ranch that are "cutting edge" are the most important... the information, the approach and the teachers.

We will give you the tools, the information and the methods that can transform your entire pitching game. Of course, there are a few things that are expected from you (and a few principles that we expect our pitchers to embrace)...

- We **expect your absolute best** – no exceptions

- We hold you accountable for your movements, thoughts and behaviors

- We **guide, support, inspire** and paint a picture of the possible

- We are completely different from the traditional or conventional and we make no excuses or apologies for our uniqueness

- **We believe God is great and through Him...absolutely anything is possible**. There is no place on Earth more optimistic and positive with regards to developing the throwing athlete than the Texas Baseball Ranch and Pitching Central

For more information or to purchase a Boot Camp:

www.PitchingWithConfidence.com

NOTES

Coach Wolforth's

Multimedia Personalized At Home Pitcher Training Process

Coach Wolforth Analyzing The Movements of Professional Pitchers Trevor Bauer (Right) of the Arizona Diamondbacks and Mike Boyden (Left) of the Washington Nationals on his iPad.

Most Athletes Don't Plan to Fail- They Simply Fail to Have a Plan

The 3 Reasons 98.2% Athletes FAIL to Reach Their God Given Potential

#1- Lack of a Clear Vision- They are uncertain on exactly what to do and/or how to do it.

153

#2- Lack of a Coherent High Quality Plan- They don't have a specific plan to make necessary improvements.

#3- Lack of Follow Through- They get discouraged and or frustrated and stop before they reach their dreams.

"Coach Wolforth's Multimedia Personalized At Home Training Process™ is the most complete, most comprehensive and most personalized training program for the pitching athlete in the world today. For several years I researched every process and bought almost every program. Coach Wolforth has made the world of difference for my son over the past 3 years. The very best thing is that although we live over 13 hours and 800 miles from Coach, he is our personal pitching coach every single day of the year. Instead of having to depend on finding a competent local pitching guy, we've got the very best in the business. THAT is huge."

Jack Sells, father of a 12-year-old pitcher, Nashville, TN

154

The Conventional Path= Conventional Results

A vast majority of pitchers have a personal pitching coach, take lessons or have some form of a mentor.

A few of these men are exceptionally helpful and are indeed difference makers. A vast, vast majority of them however are good men with great intentions but their opinions, theories, strategies and techniques simply make little difference to the performance of the pitching athlete. And unfortunately, a significant portion of these instructors actually take players backward or place them at greater risk of injury.

What Research Tells Us About Instruction

In our over 20 years of experience training pitching athletes we have found that most pitching athletes take one lesson a week from their instructor. The average lesson fee in the US and Canada is $64 per one hour lesson. Therefore, the typical parent will spend a little more than $240 per month on instruction for 4-5 months of the year. That equates to around $1000 per year for pitching instruction. The average pitcher trains for 4.9 years from the age of 11 until they are a junior in high school and either they are on track for a college scholarship or they quit pitching.

What exactly do you get for your $64?

So what does the typical parent get for their investment?
Well, let's look at what the typical lesson affords the
average pitcher.

The typical lesson goes something like this:

- A general warm-up
- A few lead up drills
- Verbal instruction given while performing drills like:
  "Get your elbow up", "pause at the top", "finish
  your pitch"
- Finish with a 15-50 pitch bull pen from a mound
- Some more verbal instruction and guidelines to
  keep in mind for upcoming games

Does this sound 'exceptional' to you?

The typical results: Because they basically do what
everybody else is doing, they get just about what
everybody else gets, which isn't much.

From 1995 until 2003, Coach Wolforth managed such a
typical facility. It was called the CAN-AM baseball/softball
academy. The academy performed over 800 lessons every
month. CAN-AM was located in the greater Houston, Texas
area and built a great reputation over those 8 years.
However Coach Wolforth was not satisfied with the results
and became obsessed with creating exponentially better
results by continually improving the training process.

The Texas Baseball Ranch is Born

Coach and his wife Jill purchased 20 acres of land just outside beautiful Montgomery, Texas and built the Texas Baseball Ranch. Since 2003, The Texas Baseball Ranch™ has become the number one pitching facility in the world, producing 64 drafted athletes and 114 athletes who have topped 90mph. Coach Wolforth created those results by mastering seven key elements he found to be critical in developing the 'complete' pitching athlete.

Coach Wolforth's Training Process has seven key elements:

1. Physical Assessment – much like a car with tires out of balance, wheels misaligned or one tire flat, the human body performs far better when it is balanced, aligned and free of injury. Coach's system assists you in asking all the right questions and finding the right answers with regards to physical alignment, asymmetries and strength imbalances. On page 17 in this book, Coach gives you a glimpse into the importance he places upon physical assessment.

2. Mechanical Efficiency- this is SO much more than 'mechanics'. Read Coach's Chapter 5 on mechanics to get a sense of the detail and complexity of human movement. You can see immediately why having Coach as your personal mentor is the way to go if you are truly serious about pitching as a skill. His knowledge on this subject is both wide and deep.

3. Specific Skill Measurement- the saying if you want to improve something, find a way to measure it, is a driving force for both Coach Wolforth and The Texas Baseball Ranch. You will simply be amazed by how many specific ways Coach measures and tracks performance and skill development. The Ranch is considered the world's unquestioned leader in the objective measurement of pitching skill. In fact several NCAA programs and MLB organization have come to The Ranch to study and learn the process of how The Ranch measures skill development.

4. Skill Specific Strength (BBM)- it's not enough simply to get stronger. As a pitching athlete, you will want to get stronger SPECIFICALLY to your skill. Chapter 10 does a good job in detailing what Coach believes is involved in building strength specific to pitching a baseball at a world class level. Most pitchers waste their time in gyms or worse yet, actually do things which ultimately will interfere with their performance. That simply does not happen to a Ranch pitcher following this process.

5. Nutrition/ Hydration/Sleep/Recovery/ Lifestyle- while these things seem simple and straightforward, so often they are missed or taken for granted. Coach places you on a path where you can easily stay on track and make these things work for you and become a strength and not become a distraction or a limitation.

6. Mindset/ Mental / Emotional- This element is Coach's passion. He believes everything starts and ends with mindset. For the past 7 years Coach has started EVERY session with his clients with a segment on mindset. In fact he is now sought out as a presenter by the corporate world because they see how powerful his mindset segments are. One of coach's many mantras is 'If you have a big enough why....the how will become self-evident.' If you are truly going to become 'so good no one can ignore you', Coach Wolforth's mindset segments will be invaluable.

7. Spiritual- Coach often says, "We are spiritual beings having a physical experience. Therefore any path we choose will be so much deeper and more meaningful if we embrace and develop universal spiritual principles such as appreciation, compassion, courage, honor, integrity, honesty, self-discipline, responsibility, friendship, perseverance and loyalty."

After 5 years of testing and development, in 2012, Coach designed a Multimedia / Online version of his training process so athletes living anywhere internet access was available could actually be trained by the Texas Baseball Ranch™. After 20 years of work and developing pitchers, Coach realized that the very best way to create a pitching athlete so good that no one could ignore them was to make certain he was developing the TOTAL pitching athlete. Coach witnessed firsthand time and time again that a breakdown in ANY one of the seven areas could stop an athlete dead in his tracks. In essence, having good mechanics was FAR from enough to create excellence, in fact it was just ONE piece of the puzzle. To be great, the athlete needed to develop the complete package.

While that makes perfect sense to most people, the real question is exactly how do you do this? Exactly how does one systematically eat this huge 'elephant' one piece at a time? And that is the brilliance of Coach's system.

The Genius of Coach Wolforth's At Home and Online Training System

Coach designed his process following the 3000 year old systematic martial arts model of colored belts.

Each athlete will begin at White, which is Level 1. He will pass out of each of the 7 elements in Level I with either a written test and a video analysis. Level I is designed to be mastered in 4 weeks. When the athlete passes out of each of the 7 elements of Level I, the athlete can then graduate to the next, more challenging level. The process is so well structured and so developmentally appropriate that even Coach's professional pitching clients follow the exact process.

As Coach likes to say, 'Skills and competencies are best built upon one another like building blocks. Before one can run, one should always learn to crawl and walk first. Pitching a baseball is no different. I see many of my professional clients fail to perform simple fundamental movement patterns of healthy deceleration and subsequently they pay the price for such inefficiency in terms of labrum surgery and shoulder and elbow issues. No one escapes fundamental mechanical inefficiencies for long. Our goal is to master basic movement fundamentals as soon as possible and begin as soon as possible to reap the benefits of a healthy, durable, electric arm.'

Coach has six additional levels including Yellow, Green, Orange, Red, Blue and eventually Black, which denotes 'elite mastery'. Each level the athlete masters, Coach rewards the athlete by specific gifts from The Ranch commensurate with each level. As the levels go higher, the rewards grow in significance.

As a special gift for reading the book, Coach will offer any athlete to get started on Level I absolutely for free. Simply go to the website **www.RonWolforthBaseballTraining.com** and type in the promotional code "Survival Guide" and follow along with the process.

We believe once you experience the way Ron Wolforth's Texas Baseball Ranch™ trains its pitchers, you will no longer accept the standard, conventional path of weekly lessons. You will choose a different path. As Coach Wolforth loves to say, 'You cannot be common for common men go nowhere. You must be uncommon.' Coach Wolforth's Multimedia Personalized At Home Training Process™ represents the most advanced, accelerated and comprehensive process of training pitchers in the world today. If you are looking for the fastest, safest and surest route to becoming so good that others simply can't ignore you, this is the process for you.

"We became involved with Coach Wolforth when my son was 8 and he didn't even have a delivery or throw it 45 mph. Now 3 years later my son is an elite select ball pitcher throwing 64 mph and more importantly has an incredibly healthy and durable arm. Something that I assure you is rare among youth select pitchers. We are spoiled. We STARTED with Coach. I cannot more highly recommend Coach Wolforth and his training. It is logical. It is comprehensive. It is systematic. It's made personally to fit each athlete and it is life changing. My son is simply a better person because of the training. No matter what happens in the future with my son's baseball, you can't put a price tag on that. We are in ALL the way to the black belt."

Max Soliz,
Houston, Texas

Coach Wolforth's

Multimedia Personalized At Home Pitcher Training Process

www.RonWolforthBaseballTraining.com

To Get More Information and to Request a Training Application Contact the Texas Baseball Ranch:

Ron Wolforth's Texas Baseball Ranch
5451 Honea-Egypt Road
Montgomery, Tx 77316

Phone: (936) 588-6762
Fax: (281) 298-7391
Email: info@TexasBaseballRanch.com

Also Available from Coach Wolforth
- Membership Programs
- At-Home Training Products
- Online training
- Exclusive Boot camps
- Personal One on one coaching
- Speaking

For More Information on these Products Visit:
- www.PitchingCentral.com
- www.PitchingWithConfidence.com
- www.TexasBaseballRanch.com

"Failure is simply the opportunity to begin again, this time more intelligently."

Henry Ford

Made in the USA
Charleston, SC
13 March 2013